The Legacy of Jawaharlal Nehru

By the same author
—How Relevant is Gandhi Today?: A Japanese View

About the Author

H. Yamaguchi studied at the University of Tokyo, and got his B.A. and M.A. degrees in sociology. He worked at the IDE (Institute of Developing Economies, a semi-governmental research organization), then taught at Bunkyo University, both Tokyo-based. He was a Writer-in-Residence at the Mahatma Gandhi International Hindi University, Wardha, in 2005.

Yamaguchi's primary research interest may be termed the human factor in development, with his major regional moorings in India. His contact with India goes back to Jawaharlal Nehru's Prime Ministerial times. His secondary academic interest is modern Japan's relations with Asian nations.

Although his writings have been mostly in Japanese, he has co-edited *Tradition and Modernity: India and Japan towards the Twenty-first Century* (Munshiram Manoharlal, 1997), and written *Japan* (National Book Trust, India, 2006). He has participated in a number of academic conferences held in India, starting from "Nehru as Writer and Historian", sponsored by NMML, in 1989.

The Legacy of Jawaharlal Nehru

A Japanese View

Yamaguchi Hiroichi

CONCEPT PUBLISHING COMPANY PVT. LTD.
NEW DELHI-110059

ISBN-13: 978-93-88937-10-8

First Published 2019

Published and Printed by:

Since 1974

Concept Publishing Company Pvt. Ltd.
A/15-16, Commercial Block, Mohan Garden,
New Delhi-110059 (INDIA)
T : 91 11 25351460, 91 11 25351794
E : publishing@conceptpub.com, *W* : www.conceptpub.com

Cataloging in Publication Data--Courtesy: D.K. Agencies (P) Ltd. <docinfo@dkagencies.com>

Yamaguchi, Hiroichi, author.
The legacy of Jawaharlal Nehru : a Japanese view / Yamaguchi Hiroichi.
pages cm
Includes bibliographical references and index.
ISBN 9789388937108

1. Nehru, Jawaharlal, 1889-1964. 2. India—Politics and government—20th century. I. Title.

LCC DS481.N35Y36 2019 | DDC 954.035 23

Preface

This author, out of his conviction that Mahatma Gandhi is still relevant in this world, perhaps more so today than before, has published *How Relevant Is Gandhi Today? A Japanese View* from the Concept Publishing Co. (P) Ltd., in 2015. Subsequently, he came to entertain the view that now that a book on the *guru* is out a book on the disciples, more or less in consonance with the first one, may be called for. This small book is the outcome of that work on the disciples, particularly on one of them and perhaps the most remarkable of them, Jawaharlal Nehru. This is also an attempt to measure the contemporary significance, or the relevance, or the legacies, of this man. Nehru has been selected because, as is the case with Gandhi, or even more so, there have not been many works on him worth pondering on in recent years. Someone has rightly said that there are fewer biographies of Nehru than he deserves. Moreover, it seems to be increasingly difficult unfortunately to openly discuss him in India these days.

In the following pages the author would call his Gandhi book, mentioned above, as the previous book or the earlier book. It means not just the chronological order, but the basic continuity of the two books. In the basic evaluation of Gandhi the author's thinking has not changed from the first one, and what appears in this second one is really based on the first. The author even would like to take it for granted that the basic ideas on Gandhi shown in the first one have been accepted by the readers, and the author will continue on that path and build on it.

He may be allowed to say one thing here on his attitude in facing Gandhi or Nehru. When a friend of his in Eastern India has read the first book, on Gandhi, he sent an email to the author saying that he has found the author "neither a devotee nor a harsh critic of Gandhi". He means he likes it. That has greatly pleased the author as that is how it should be. In the following pages also he would try to be like that.

Acknowledgements

When interviewing an Indian on Gandhi, it may be natural that some other persons have also come into the conversation. This particularly applies to Jawaharlal Nehru. It would not make sense to meet the same person twice and to interview him on Gandhi for the first time and on Nehru for the second. Therefore, the author is not making a separate list for acknowledgements for this book, different from the earlier one, and would like to offer the list of about 65 Indian names acknowledged in the first book as one for this book also.

Among the Japanese, just as the author has mentioned the one name of Tanaka Toshio in the earlier book, in this one he would like to thank particularly Nakamura Heiji, a Professor Emeritus of the Tokyo University of Foreign Studies and a pioneer in the study of the Modern South Asian Political History in Japan for many years by now. Especially, the author would like to express his thanks to him for the encouragement he has given to us by publishing a biography of Nehru (in Japanese) as early as in 1966, more than half a century ago. This is practically the only work on Nehru in the book form in the post-Second World War Japan.

Contents

Introduction

Like the previous book, this book also aims at a comprehensive study of Nehru and not his biography. But what are to be its main focuses on Nehru ?

First, what is the relation of Gandhi and Nehru? Gandhi, who knew the difference between himself and Nehru, used to say that after him Nehru would speak his language. But did Nehru really ? Usually secularism, parliamentary democracy, economic planning, Hindu Code Bill and the like are listed as Nehru's legacies. But does it mean Nehru spoke Gandhi's language? Did Nehru think much of, for example, primary education, or primary health care, and the like? Did not Nehru depend more and more on the bureaucracy and that much less on the mass initiative and the mass movement?

Second, what is the historic significance of the Indo-China War of 1962? What is most difficult to write about Nehru is how India and China went to war in 1962 and what Nehru's role in it was. Part of the difficulty arises because the *Selected Writings of Jawaharlal Nehru (Second Series)* is not yet complete, having come out up to Vol.70 as of writing, covering only up to August 1961. The rest of nearly three years of his life not yet covered by those volumes includes the whole period of the War. Therefore, the author feels on one hand like waiting for at least several, maybe more, volumes to come out covering this crucial period of his life directly leading to the end of it. It is really the ambition of the author to be the first researcher to study the entire writings of Nehru and incorporate them into his work. But on the other hand he is not at all sure, if that will be possible. What is at stake is not only his role in the War itself. What Nehru ordered or directed in this period must have bound the subsequent attitudes and policies of the Government of India to a great extent. Therefore, the author has decided not to wait for the completion of Nehru's writings, and to cover the vacuum by other material as much as possible. Part of this discussion concerning the historic significance of the war and its aftermath will be seen in the Epilogue. The author would be more than happy if in the future he may be able to make it up by more orthodox means.

Third, what is Japan's place in connection with Nehru? As in the previous one, here are also attached the words "A Japanese View". For one thing we take note of Nehru's deep interest in Japan, not only in his capacity as a politician and diplomat, but also his interest in Japan's culture and history. As far as we the Japanese are concerned, because of Nehru's visit to Japan in 1957, and its timeliness which will be discussed later, he was rather more familiar than Gandhi to the ordinary Japanese people. This is in spite of his strong anti-Japanese and anti-imperialist nationalistic activities during the War years. At the same time, it is worth knowing how Indo-Japanese relations have changed after Nehru and why? To that extent it is a part of the Nehru legacy. The discussion on this point, which will also be made in the Epilogue, will bring us to the present day.

Two points may be mentioned. We will call our hero simply as Nehru, or if necessary as Jawaharlal Nehru, instead of more popular usages in India like Jawaharlal or Panditji. Secondly, we use SWJN-1, SWJN-2, and LCM for the *Selected Works of Jawaharlal Nehru*, *Selected Works of Jawaharlal Nehru (Second Series)*, and *Letters to Chief Ministers*, respectively, and the references to these three will be noted in the text itself with the volume numbers and pages. Other references will be made in the Notes.

1
Nehru's Background

Three Books

This is not Nehru's biography. This is a study of his thought and behaviour in their basic features. We have not traced his life moment by moment. However, the minimum of his career and the way of thinking should be tried to be given here so that it will become possible to know him deeper.

During his long political life, even up to India's independence, he was imprisoned nine times, totalling 3,262 days. On one summer day in 1945 he was finally released from the Almora Jail as the freedom had come nearer. Economist P.C. Joshi, who is from the area and who happened to meet Nehru walking down the hills fresh from the Jail, vividly narrated the encounter to the author when he interviewed Joshi in 2003. Pointing to one of the Himalayan peaks, Nehru asked him "Young man, what is the name of that mountain?".

Three times out of these nine imprisonments, Nehru wrote a book, altogether three. They are *Glimpses of World History*, *An Autobiography*, and *The Discovery of India*. These were big and great books which not only became well-known worldwide, but they represent Nehru very well in one way or another. They are not academic books, or have been written systematically. They are more or less meant for general readers. That is all the more reason why the study of these books will be useful in understanding the general approach of Nehru to the past, present and the future of India and mankind in general.

Therefore, one of the best ways to know him, at least in his initial stages, until he became mature, and even the first Prime Minister of a great country, is to look at each of these three books closely and find out what is lurking behind them. This is what we are going to do in this initial Chapter.

Incidentally, these three have all been translated into Japanese and are, therefore, fairly widely known in Japan as well.

So, we will talk about those three books by taking them up one by one chronologically.

Glimpses of World History

This was the first of the three, and is the most voluminous as well, exceeding 1,100 pages in its currently available Penguin edition. It is a collection of the letters he wrote to his daughter Indira on the evolution of the history of mankind as a part of her education, who had been deprived of the opportunity of regularly attending educational institutions. It is astonishing the way he collects materials from all over the world history, the East and the West, the ancient and the modern, so that he may impress the reader with the idea that the human history is moving ahead, however slowly it may seem.

There are 196 letters in the book. The first one was dated New Year's Day, 1931. This was when Nehru was in prison because of the Salt March. He was at the end of his thirties then.

Most of the letters were written during 'a long spell' (M.J. Akbar) in prison. The last one was dated 9 August, 1933. The main reader, Indira, had been born in 1917.

There is a fairly long Postscript to the book which was written on 14 November, 1938 when Nehru was free and was on the 'Arabian Sea' on his way back from Europe. He became 49 on this day. There he writes briefly "the story of these five years", touching upon Abyssinia, Spain, China, Austria, Czechoslovakia, Russia, Economic Recovery, The British Empire, Colonies, America, Turkey, Islam, and The World in Conflict. It is clear from the above that he was anticipating the Second World War as a fight between Fascism and Democracy, though he was not so clear on the way India would be affected by or involved in that War.

We will look into some of the impressive letters to know his way of thinking.

Nehru held a firm belief in the basic cultural integrity and continuity of India. He wrote "The Aryans and the Dravidians gave much to each other and took much from each other also, and thus built up a common culture for India."[1] In a similar tone he wrote on Shankara that "Another fact which Shankara's brief but strenuous life brings out is the cultural unity of India."[2] In such an India, "It is strange that anyone should be so foolish as to think that religion and faith can be thrust down a person's throat at the point of the sword or a bayonet."[3] Likewise, "unhappily, we have had religious and communal troubles recently, and some people, ignorant of history, imagine that this has been India's fate right through the ages. This is wholly wrong. Such troubles are largely of recent growth. You will find that after Islam began, for many hundred years Musalmans lived in all parts of India in perfect peace with their neighbours. They were welcomed when they came as traders and encouraged to settle down."[4]

It would be interesting how he has described China and its people in view of the many things that have taken place between the two countries later on. He compares China with Japan. "The Chinese people have been and are an essentially peaceful people. The whole of their civilization and philosophy of life is peaceful. The Japanese, on the other hand, have been and still are a fighting people."[5] He further says, and this is very penetrating. "Thus, we see that although modern China entered more into the spirit of Western civilization, Japan outstripped her because she put on the armour of it, ignoring the spirit. And all Europe praised Japan because she was strong in this armour, and they made her one of their fellowship."[6] Rabindranath Tagore once said something similar to this.

Coming back to India, at the age of Babar, Nehru says that "It is interesting to note that the whole of India was looked upon as a unit by Babar, although when he came it was split up into many kingdoms. This idea of the unity of India has persisted throughout history."[7] At the same time his comments on Akbar were "In a sense he might be considered to be the father of Indian nationalism. At a time when there was little of nationality in the country and religion was a dividing factor, Akbar deliberately placed the ideal of a common Indian nationhood above the claims of separatist religion."[8]

Nehru also discusses the historical decay in the Indian economy. "There is no question of a practical and materialistic West and a spiritual and other-worldly East. The difference is between an industrial and highly mechanized West, with all its accompanying good and bad points, and an East, which is still largely pre-industrial and agricultural."[9] And "Some people say that the East is spiritual and the West material. This kind of remark is very deceptive. The real difference between the East and the West at the time when Europe came as aggressor, in the eighteenth and nineteenth centuries, was the medievalism of the East and the industrial and mechanical progress of the West."[10] What was the distance between India and Europe at the time, then? "India was in a transition stage. It was a manufacturing country, and a *bourgeois* class was being evolved in these towns. The owners of these factories were capitalists who supplied raw material to the craftsmen. In course of time this class would no doubt have grown powerful enough, as in Europe, to replace the feudal class. Just then the British intervened, with fatal results to India's industries."[11] It seems Nehru was thus of the view that there was a universal law of capitalist development in the world, and the difference was simply a matter of time. "India actually went back as a result of British policy. She ceased even to be a manufacturing country, and became, more than ever, an agricultural country."[12]

On the relations of different communities within this historical tragedy, Nehru writes on Bengal that "In Bengal, which has the biggest Muslim population of any Indian province, they were poor tenants or small land-holders. The landlord was usually a Hindu, and so was the village *bania*, who was the money-lender and the owner of the village store. The landlord and the *bania* were thus in a position to oppress the tenant and exploit him, and they took full advantage of this position. It is well to remember this fact, for in this lies the root cause of the tension between Hindu and Muslim."[13] Thus, Nehru does not attribute the Hindu-Muslim conflict to the religious factor as such.

Nehru tried to learn the lessons from the experiences of some of the countries in the Middle East. Let us see what they were. When Kemal Pasha became victorious in the war over his Turkish motherland after the end of the First World War, "He had given up all ideas of Turkish dominion over non-Turkish lands like Arabia and Iraq and Palestine and Syria."[14] Apart from the question of who took control of those areas, their abandonment necessarily put the Sultanate and the Caliphate, especially the latter, into question. A greater contradiction for the Indians at the time was the fact that in India both Hindus and Muslims were gradually mobilized in the Khilafat Movement under the initiative of Gandhi, though there were some intellectuals, as will be discussed elsewhere in this book, who had taken keen interest in the nationalistic sentiment among those non-Turkish people. We may count Nehru among them also which is a very important characteristic of him.

Nehru then wrote on the exchange of population that took place involving Turkey. "Some years later, at Greek suggestion, an extraordinary exchange of populations took place. The remaining Greeks in Anatolia were sent over to Greece, and in exchange Turks from Greece were brought over. About a million and a half Greeks were thus exchanged, and most of these families had lived for generations and centuries in Anatolia and Greece respectively. It was an amazing uprooting of peoples, and it completely upset the economic life of Turkey, especially as the Greeks had a great share in commerce."[15] In 1933, when this letter was written, Nehru was of course not in a position to anticipate an at least equally amazing uprooting of peoples in his own home country a little more than a decade later. But, it seems no one, let alone Nehru himself, had thought of this historical precedent at the time of the partition.

But, it was more, perhaps much more, to Egypt than Turkey, that Nehru paid his attention, as he wrote himself that "For us in India there is an especial lesson, for we can see, in the example of Egypt, what British grants of "freedom" amount to, and what they lead to."[16]

When Britain made a unilateral declaration in 1922, and said that in future Egypt would be an independent sovereign state, they also said that there would be attached four conditions and one of them was the protection of minorities. So far, it looks almost like in India. But, there was a great difference, not in the British policy but in the people's response. According to Nehru, "The chief minority was that of the Copts...Soon after the British declaration of February 1922, the Copts gathered together at a great meeting and resolved "that they renounce all minority representation and minority protection in the interest of national unity and the attainment of the national aim."[17] The Copts' position was comparable to that of the Indian Muslims as they were Christians and as such a religious minority among the Muslim majority. But here on this occasion they chose to go a very different way from the Indian Muslims.

Nehru also watched the emerging trouble in Palestine. He said that when Britain made the Balfour Declaration to establish a "Jewish National Home" in Palestine in 1917, the same year as the Montagu's declaration for India, "Palestine was not a wilderness, or an empty, uninhabited place. It was already somebody else's home."[18] He also says that "This shows that the real trouble was not religious, but economic conflict between the newcomers and the old residents."[19]

Finally, we will notice that Nehru, probably in one of the first, and far-sighted attempts in the world to do so, talked about the unemployed, or dispossessed, middle class in Italy and Germany to join the Fascist forces in their countries.[20]

To Nehru himself, as he wrote in his *An Autobiography*, "My historical series of letters to my daughter kept me occupied right through my two-year term, and they helped me very greatly to keep mentally fit."[21] At this time his only intended reader was a mere teen-ager. But, as is clear from the above, what he has written is more, may be much more, than what that reader may have been in need of at that time.

An Autobiography

This second one was written during the next long spell in prison from 1934 to 1935. Historian S. Gopal says in his biography of Nehru that this was the first narrative of Asian nationalism, and the best work by Nehru. The famous Congress-League Scheme of 1916 at Lucknow, we are told, had been 'drawn up' at the AICC meeting held at his house at Allahabad.[22] It is a bit of a surprise that an increasingly greater part of Nehru's activities became concerned with the peasant movement. "I was thrown, almost without any will of my own, into contact with the peasantry."[23] This was when in the beginning of June 1920 about 200 peasants came walking to Allahabad all the way, and at their request Nehru spent three days at their villages, among the "naked, starving, crushed, and utterly miserable" India, mostly ejected landless people, as in Oudh there were no occupancy tenants or even life tenants, only short-term tenants.[24] Nehru later adds that "tenants are far more numerous than peasant proprietors."[25] Ramachandra who took the peasants to Nehru was what Rajkumar was for Gandhi at Champaran, Bihar.

In the Khilafat Movement which came up almost simultaneously, Nehru saw: "The influence and prestige of the Moulvies...began to grow again and dominate the Muslim community", and "I did not like it at all."[26] Because of this, the nationalism of India became "a composite force, and behind it could be distinguished a Hindu nationalism, a Muslim nationalism...and...an Indian nationalism."[27] Moreover, "The Sikhs were now loudly advancing their communal demands, and an extraordinarily complicated triangle was created in the Punjab. The Punjab, indeed, became the crux of the matter."[28] It remained so till the partition.

Motilal Nehru, his father, and a fearful lawyer, although politically liberal, became very close to Gandhi. Even politically, among the veteran leaders of the Congress, "my father was the only one to take his stand by Gandhiji at that time."[29] He was talking of the crucial Special Congress Session at Calcutta in September 1920 to discuss Gandhi's proposal for Non-cooperation. Much later, when Motilal was critically ill, Gandhi remained at his bedside, and was also to be seen at the cremation. Motilal had said to Gandhi a few days before his demise, "I am going soon, Mahatmaji...I shall not be here to see *Swaraj*. But I know that you have won it and will soon have it."[30]

In the second half of 1920s Nehru made an extended tour of Europe with his family, including Motilal. This made him of sterner stuff in the sense that he now thought of "social freedom and a socialistic structure of society and the State."[31] as essential over and above political independence. To that extent he was now a socialist.

Around this time Nehru wrote a short essay titled "The Situation in China and India's Duty". It was his first writing on China, where he wrote that "the use of Indian troops in China" etc. was bound to "tarnish the good name of India" (SWJN-1, 2-326-8).

Back at home he succeeded his father as the Congress President at its Lahore Session in the end of 1929. He said in his Presidential Address on 29 December that "I must frankly confess that I am a socialist and a republican. We have three major problems—the minorities, the Indian states, and labour and peasantry" (SWJN-1, 4-184-198). He concluded his address with '*Vande Mataram*'.

The Salt March of March to April 1930 started the Civil Disobedience Movement. But Gandhi's own fast on the Communal Award in September 1932 was "the first severe blow" to it, and it was "finally killed for all practical purposes by the suspension of it in May 1933."[32] Nehru sounds a little (or not a little) cynical on his *guru's* attitude toward the main goal of CD.

On the Hindu-Muslim relations Nehru makes some important comments. He says, "Latterly there has been an interesting development in the speeches and statements of some of the Muslim communal leaders...Stress has been laid on the 'Muslim nation' in India, on 'Muslim culture', on the utter incompatibility of Hindu and Muslim 'cultures' ."[33] The author wonders if Nehru has taken those speeches and statements sufficiently seriously and faced them squarely as an adversary ideology.

The narrative comes up to 14 February, 1935. There is a Postscript telling us that his wife, Kamala, is recuperating in Europe and Nehru himself has been discharged and left to join her.

These are followed by "Five Years Later". Kamala died at Lausanne in February 1936. Nehru had to come home as he had been elected Congress President shortly before. He soon thought of resigning as he had trouble in coordinating his policies with his Working Committee colleagues. He had included three socialists—Narendra Deva, Jayaprakash Narayan (hereafter JP), and Achyut Patwardhan—among the thirteen members of his Committee. But news of rebellion against a legally elected government from Spain changed his mind. Then, "This public interest was kept up by thousands of meetings and demonstrations that the Congress organized all over the country in sympathy with the people of China, Abyssinia, Palestine and Spain."[34]

There were also the first provincial elections under the new 1935 Government of India Act, and the campaign became "a memorable affair" for him and "a voyage of discovery of India and her people."[35] He especially mentions his sister, Vijaya Lakshmi Pandit, as the first woman provincial Minister in India, and it is as if he is recommending her name as his successor, at least in their home province of Uttar Pradesh.

After serving two terms as Congress President, he made a short visit to Europe. "I entered into this Europe of conflict by flying straight to Barcelona. There I remained for five days and watched the bombs fall nightly from the air."[36] So, he was actually bombed! Later, he was bombed by the Japanese while visiting China, but that is not narrated in the book. The Postscript mentioned before, written in 1938, to his

Glimpses of World History, must have been written on his way home from this European tour.

Nehru's letter to his close friend V.K. Krishna Menon of 6 August, 1936, just after the Spanish Civil War had started, is worth reading as it shows his wide grasp of things and far-sightedness. It says "For the present however interest goes but to the happenings in Spain and to the great influence they are likely to have on the future shaping of events in Europe and the world" (SWJN-1, 7-576). He made 9 May of that year Abyssinia Day, 27 September Palestine Day, and 26 September, 1937 and 9 January, 1938 China Day.

Just prior to the Second World War, Nehru made a thirteen-day trip to China at the end of August 1939. He wrote about it in "Diary of a Journey", which was included in *China, Spain and the War*, a book published in 1940. He left Calcutta, and reached Chungking, China's war-time capital, *via* Saigon, Hanoi and Kunming. He spent most of his time in Chungking but visited Chungtu also. He had a plan to further go to the north to visit the Eighth Route Army and the Congress medical unit. But the war broke out in Europe and he was ordered to come home. While in Chungking he experienced air raids five times. Also at Chungking he was visited by Yeh Chienying, a Communist General. There is no record of his meeting Zhou En-lai who is supposed to have been staying in Chungking at that time as the Communist Party representative. If they had met then and made friends ? (SWJN-1,10-84-100). Mao Zedong, the Communist Party Chairman, and Zhu De, Commander-in-Chief of the Eighth Route Army, both of whom Nehru could not meet, later sent him a joint letter of thanks. It is not to be found in the SWJN-1.

Dick Wilson, British specialist on the Far Eastern Affairs, wrote in his *Chou The Story of Zhou Enlai 1898-1976* on Zhou in Chungking at this time as follows. "Zhou seized every opportunity to establish relations with other countries, from Korea to India. He regretted missing Jawaharlal Nehru when he made a visit to the Chinese capital, and indeed this was a lost opportunity of some consequence. If these Asian nationalist leaders, comparable in so many ways, had formed a mutual understanding and liking at this stage, when neither was burdened with the responsibilities of government, the Sino-Indian antagonism of twenty years later might have been avoided."[37] By contrast Han Suyin, another biographer of Zhou, did not discuss in her book any such possibility of these two leaders meeting at the war-time Capital Chungking. We will refer to her work later.

The War started and it involved India against her wishes. There was a serious parting of ways between Gandhi and most of the Working Committee members on the problem of war-time non-violence, in other words whether to help the British to fight the war or not, the former group including Nehru. On 8 August, 1940 the British replied to the Congress demand in the form of the so-called "August Offer", to the bitter disappointment of the former group. *An Autobiography* concludes with that disappointment.[38]

The Discovery of India

Finally, Nehru wrote *The Discovery of India* in prison during the five months of 1944, though he was there much longer this time, from 1942 to 1945. It was by far the longest prison term for him, but, as "The night is long that never finds the day", it proved to be his last as well.

He had already written the world history and the autobiography. There remains the Indian history. This is what he had in mind. He put it in such questions as "What is my inheritance? To what am I an heir?"[39], or "What is this India, apart from her physical and geographical aspects?"[40]

Therefore, it is a history book, so it is interesting that the woman of India is the subject matter of its chapter 2. There Nehru writes, "Most of us menfolk were in prison. And then a remarkable thing happened. Our women came to the front and took charge of the struggle...which took not only the British Government but their own menfolk by surprise."[41] Then he touched on Kamala, whose death we already knew in *An Autobiography*. He says, "In this upheaval Kamala had played a brave and notable part and on her inexperienced shoulders fell the task of organizing our work in the city of Allahabad when every known worker was in prison."[42]

"*The Discovery of India*" is also the title of chapter 4 of this book, but we have seen that the phrase was already used in connection with his election campaign in his previous book. The chapter, the first substantial one of the book, starts from the Indus Valley Civilization and comes up to Ashoka, who proclaimed that "All sects deserve reverence for one reason or another."[43] According to Nehru, "Unlike the Greeks, and unlike the Chinese and the Arabs, Indians in the past were not historians. This was very unfortunate and it has made it difficult for us now to fix dates or make up an accurate chronology."[44] The land-tax was about one-sixth of the produce.[45] Perhaps in some historical continuity Vinoba Bhave's *Bhoodan* Movement invited the landlords to give one-sixth of their land. Back in the ancient history "Widow remarriage is recognized; also divorce under certain circumstances."[46] Also, "In Indian polity if the king is unjust or tyrannical, the right to rebel against him is admitted."[47] It is somewhat similar to the Chinese political philosophy.

Down the ages, Nehru sounds a bit critical of the nature of the Indian society. Here is, for example, a very sharp comment. "It is interesting to note that while Indian philosophy is highly individualistic and deals almost entirely with individual's growth to some kind of inner perfection, the Indian social structure was communal and paid attention to groups only. The individual was allowed perfect freedom to think and believe what he liked, but he had to conform strictly to social and communal usage."[48] "This structure was based on three concepts—the autonomous village community, caste, and the joint family system."[49] "All the three pillars of the Indian social structure were thus based on the group and not on the individual."[50] Under these circumstances, "as a rule, conversions to Islam were group conversions, so powerful was the influence of the group...Because of this we find today particular occupations and crafts almost entirely monopolized by Muslims."[51] It was said that with the departure of many Muslim residents from Delhi and elsewhere for Pakistan at the time of the partition, workers of some particular crafts were completely gone, leaving India that much simpler and poorer in social composition.

Nehru continued to say how the Indian society is handicapped in other ways also. He says that "The emphasis of Jainism and Buddhism on non-violence led to the tilling of the soil being considered a lowly occupation, for it often resulted in the destruction of animal life."[52] He also quotes a high priest from China who spent many years in India, perhaps in seventh century, saying that "the peculiar distinction between purity and impurity" is characteristic of the Indian culture.[53]

Nehru, however, also emphasizes the spirit of tolerance in the

Indian society, particularly with reference to the Hindu-Muslim relations. When Islam came to India, "There was no objection raised either by the state or the people, nor were there any religious conflicts. It was the old tradition of India to be tolerant to all faiths and forms of worship. Thus, Islam came as a religion to India several centuries before it came as a political force."[54] This does not mean that there was no mutual impact. "The fierce monotheism of Islam influenced Hinduism, and the vague pantheistic attitude of the Hindu had its effect on the Indian Muslim."[55] As a result, so to speak, even after Islam came "as a political force", "The Mughal dynasty became firmly established as India's own"[56], and "When Aurungzeb began...to function more as a Muslim than an Indian ruler, the Mughal Empire began to break up."[57]

We have seen that in his *Glimpses of World History* Nehru had expressed his view that in India also, as in Europe, the capitalist class would take the place of the feudal class in due course if India had been left alone by the Western powers. If left alone would the non-Western countries have proceeded the way of capitalist industrialization? This is an extremely interesting subject which has so far been actually debated heatedly on some of the non-Western countries, including Japan. Let us quote Nehru here a bit longer, but it deserves it.

"The economy of India had thus advanced to as high a stage as it could reach prior to the industrial revolution. Whether it had the seeds of further progress in it or was too much bound up with the rigid social structure, it is difficult to say. It seems quite possible, however, that under normal conditions it would have undergone that change and begun to adapt itself, in its own way, to the new industrial conditions...As it happened, foreign political domination came first and this led to a rapid destruction of the economy India had built up, without anything positive or constructive taking its place."[58] Thus, Nehru was of the view that India was on the threshold of an industrial revolution if left alone to herself, had there been no British interference. No doubt he had a high evaluation of what the Indian economy had achieved by then.

The chapters 7, 8, and 9 were titled The Last Phase (1), (2), and (3), occupying about half of the total pages, and covered the last 100 years, starting with the discussion of the consolidation of the British rule in India. Nehru says of Bengal that "The nineteenth century produced a galaxy of brilliant Hindus in Bengal, and yet there is hardly a single Muslim Bengali leader of any note who stands out there during this period."[59] The same applies to the whole of India.[60] At the same time he points out how the British policy was anti-people, with no Departments of Agriculture, and of Commerce and Industry, before the twentieth century, and with no food policy till 1943 when a catastrophic famine assaulted Bengal.[61]

Nehru has gone into some details concerning some of the recent political issues. On the question of forming coalition governments in the provinces as the result of the 1937 elections, a proposal which was refused by the Congress, Nehru writes that "Nevertheless it is true that the consequences of it on the communal question were unfortunate and it led to a feeling of grievance and isolation among many Muslims."[62] Here, it is as if he was having a second thought. On the resignation of the Congress provincial governments after the Second World War broke out, Nehru defended the measure by writing that "if they did not resign, they would be dismissed from office.[63]

More serious was the difference between Gandhi and most of the rest of the Congress leadership concerning the war. Gandhi adhered to non-violence. Nehru said that "Gandhi could not give up the faith of a lifetime on which he had based all his activities...."[64] Nehru himself, however, was not able to bring himself to this position. He said, "At no time, so far as I am aware, was the question of non-violence considered in relation to the army, navy, or air force, or the police. It was taken for granted that its application was confined to our struggle for freedom."[65] Nehru was thus more positive in participating in the war, and this meant a break with Gandhi. For Nehru war means war in the usual sense of the word, involving fighting of the army, navy, and air force. But for Gandhi, non-violence is a faith and not such a half-hearted affair. After 22 years of training the nation in non-violence starting from the days of the Khilafat movement, Gandhi was facing this contradiction even with his closest colleagues.

It was due to this break that the historic Quit-India Resolution adopted by the AICC at Bombay on 8 August, 1942 contained such words as "to defend India and resist aggression with all the armed as well as the non-violent forces". Apparently, it has got a dual meaning.

Or rather, it makes no meaningful sense. Even for people like Nehru who were not as rigid as Gandhi on non-violence, as he wrote, "Behind it all lay an intense feeling that it was no longer possible to endure and live under foreign autocratic rule."[66] Nothing other than this has brought him to the Ahmadnagar Fort where he was writing this.

Those three books into which Nehru put a lot of his time and energy must have given us a sufficiently wide perspective to understand Nehru's background, at least up to the Second World War. But we will further explore in the next Chapter how his thought has mixed up with that of Gandhi, or otherwise.

Notes

1. Nehru, *Glimpses of World History*, 16.
2. *Ibid.*, 150.
3. *Ibid.*, 74.
4. *Ibid.*, 114.
5. *Ibid.*, 138.
6. *Ibid.*, 530.
7. *Ibid.*, 353.
8. *Ibid.*, 356-7.
9. *Ibid.*, 391-2.
10. *Ibid.*, 465.
11. *Ibid.*, 485.
12. *Ibid.*, 487.
13. *Ibid.*, 508.
14. *Ibid.*, 817.
15. *Ibid.*, 817-8.
16. *Ibid.*, 855.
17. *Ibid.*, 862.
18. *Ibid.*, 886.
19. *Ibid.*, 888.
20. *Ibid.*, 949, 1061.
21. Nehru, *An Autobiography*, 367.
22. *Ibid.*, 36.
23. *Ibid.*, 55.
24. *Ibid.*, 59.
25. *Ibid.*, 352.
26. *Ibid.*, 78-9.
27. *Ibid.*, 81.

28. *Ibid.*, 148.
29. *Ibid.*, 70.
30. *Ibid.*, 259.
31. *Ibid.*, 175.
32. *Ibid.*, 353-4.
33. *Ibid.*, 486.
34. *Ibid.*, 623-4.
35. *Ibid.*, 624-5.
36. *Ibid.*, 628.
37. Wilson, Dick, *Chou*, 156.
38. Nehru, *An Autobiography*, 636.
39. Nehru, *The Discovery of India*, 25.
40. *Ibid.*, 40.
41. *Ibid.*, 31.
42. *Ibid.*, 32.
43. *Ibid.*, 136.
44. *Ibid.*, 101.
45. *Ibid.*, 111, 272.
46. *Ibid.*, 127.
47. *Ibid.*, 267.
48. *Ibid.*, 147-8.
49. *Ibid.*, 266.
50. *Ibid.*, 275.
51. *Ibid.*, 287.
52. *Ibid.*, 185-6.
53. *Ibid.*, 207.
54. *Ibid.*, 244.
55. *Ibid.*, 262.
56. *Ibid.*, 280.
57. *Ibid.*, 286.
58. *Ibid.*, 309.
59. *Ibid.*, 349.
60. *Ibid.*, 429.
61. *Ibid.*, 362, 554.
62. *Ibid.*, 405.
63. *Ibid.*, 475.
64. *Ibid.*, 490.
65. *Ibid.*, 491-2.
66. *Ibid.*, 533.

2
Gandhi and Nehru: How They Interacted ?

Nehru and Hind Swaraj

Nehru is usually looked upon as Gandhi's disciple, even an heir. Does it mean that there was always convergence of views between the two? In the above we have already seen that actually there was a conflict of views between the two on the matter of war-time violence around 1940-42. From the study of Nehru's background on the basis of his three major works in the previous chapter, we will then examine more closely how his way overlapped or contradicted that of Gandhi. We would like to take the author's previous book *How Relevant is Gandhi Today ?* as the material for that examination.

First, how did Nehru evaluate Gandhi's writings, especially Gandhi's main work, *Hind Swaraj?*

His criticism of Gandhi first appears in his letter of 11 January, 1928 to none other than Gandhi himself, where he said that "I hardly agreed with anything that some of your previous publications—*Indian Home Rule* (*Hind Swaraj*) etc.,— contained."[1] Then in his *An Autobiography*, he writes that Gandhi is utterly wrong and harmful, his interest is in the eradication of sin from individuals, namely individual reform. He is far greater than what he writes, and he is an extraordinary paradox. He has had a fixed basis for all his ideas, and his mind is hardly an open mind.[2] All this is making it impossible for Nehru to know Gandhi through his writings, particularly after he is gone, and making him depend only on his image obtained through the direct contact while Gandhi was alive.

Did Nehru change the above view on Gandhi? It is difficult to say so. He also writes in his letter to Gandhi on 10 January, 1940 that "I have read some of your recent articles on *khadi* etc., and especially your reference to your old book *Indian Home Rule (Hind Swaraj)*. I believe in *khadi*, but I am afraid I am literally unable to accept the economic as well as other organisation of society envisaged in your book. So far as I know the Congress has never considered this, much less accepted it."[3]

Second, Gandhi is probably the only top leader of Indian nationalism who was against industrialization of India,[4] though it is true that Gandhi's critical attitude to the machines has gradually changed.[5] This has led to his criticism of Nehru's National Planning Committee before Independence. Nowhere else is clearer his opposition to the machinery than in *Hind Swaraj* when the Editor has categorically denies for India to go the way of Japan or other industrial and military powers. This was even in the excitement of the aftermath of Japan's victory in the war with Russia.

National Defence

Third, maybe as a part of the above, Gandhi gradually came against holding armed forces, and reached the conclusion of "unarmed peaceful India" as the ideal of the nation.[6] Many in the leadership of Indian nationalism, on the other hand, were all for a strong army, "a first-class military power". Nehru may have been under Gandhi's influence while he supported a relatively small army up to the war with China in 1962. But Nehru was not as a matter of principle against having a military power, which is clear from his support to the armed resistance part of the Quit-India Resolution. The August Resolution talked of "all the armed as well as the non-violent forces". This was the outcome of the compromise, sometimes nearing a break with Gandhi which had continued from the time of the August Offer in 1940.[7] Also Gandhi did not support the Indian National Army, an attempt to occupy India from outside with an armed might and in conjunction with an invading foreign power. Again he was the only such person among the top-class leaders of the Congress. As against this Nehru was one of those lawyers who defended the INA. It may be said that the difference between the two on the war and the violence involved in it had been brought out by the danger to India of the war itself.

We may see it also in Nehru's "Note on Defence" of 12 September, 1946, shortly after he had been installed as the Vice-President of the Viceroy's Executive Council, where he stresses the importance of having a national, and Indianized, army (SWJN-2, 3-488-92). Nehru, however, did a great deal in bringing about a ceasefire in the midst of the Korean War, or calling attention to the American idea of not inviting China to the Peace Conference with Japan, and of having military bases in Japan even after the Peace Treaty with her, and also in Taiwan.

Fourth, Gandhi put the idea of a decentralized Indian polity, with the residuary power vested with the provinces, in the Quit-India Resolution. It is doubtful if Nehru supported it seriously. The Constitution of the independent India, which Nehru played a great role in piloting through the Constituent Assembly, is based on a centralized Indian polity with the residuary power with the Centre.

Fifth, the Quit-India Movement has brought out some other differences between the two. Gandhi based his idea on two articles he wrote for the *Harijan* on 18 July, 1942, "To Every Japanese", and "Village Swaraj."[8] The first was a declaration to the Japanese that they should accept non-violent resistance on the part of the Indians. The second was in doing so he would give India's village republics the central place. It is difficult to imagine Nehru agreeing with either of them.

Nehru as Gandhi's Heir

Sixth, why was Nehru selected as Gandhi's heir, while Gandhi fully knew what Nehru thought of him? One reason may be that the others were not quite secular. Then Nehru had his own idea of, for example, Indian Institute of Technologies, and of English. About the differences between the two, as M. Chalapathi Rau says, they talked them over in, for example, February to March 1931. Nehru himself wrote about this in his *An Autobiography*.[9] One more important reason may be that if not Nehru, who else was there? There was only Sardar Vallabhbhai Patel who could well have been his rival otherwise but he was 14 years older than Nehru. We will see that Patel served Nehru as his Deputy very faithfully.

Seventh, but if that is so, why is it that Nehru did not take more drastic measures, broadly along the lines of, say, Arjun Sengupta Report, to raise the standard of, for example, health and education, which directly touch the life of the vast masses of the common people. This was when there were not just a few models before him for what we in the earlier one called an alternative path of development.[10] Because of the lack of progress in these areas, the common masses of people were not sure what the independence had brought, and would bring, to them in more tangible and material form. Would Gandhi not have agreed to this?

Eighth, the same can be said, perhaps with more stress, on the land problem. Gandhi and his associates had no idea of land redistribution.[11] Was Nehru also? One reason would be that Nehru and others paid more than enough respect to the "State Subjects". But would that be an enough reason? Because of this he had to depend on Vinoba Bhave's *Bhoodan* movement, but that did not produce a desired result, at least sufficiently. P. Sainath has pointed out that everybody has failed the Andhra peasant. Here Andhra must be just an example.

Bipan Chandra's Criticism

Nineth, there was important criticism by Historian Bipan Chandra of Nehru's political style in comparison with that of Gandhi. It is in two ways.

The first was what he wrote in the Chapter "Jawaharlal Nehru in Historical Perspective" in a book called *India Since Independence*, Revised and Updated in 2008, written by him and the two Mukherjees. He says that "A critical weakness of Nehru's strategy of consolidation of the Indian nation, economic development and social transformation flowed from his non-adherence to the Gandhian strategy of non-violent struggle in one crucial aspect—its emphasis on the mobilization of the people...The only form of mobilization was his extensive tours through which he communicated with the people, educated them and created popular support for his policies...The consequence was that Nehru increasingly started relying on government administration and bureaucracy for implementing his policies."[12]

His second point is that "Nehru suffered from certain economistic, deterministic and reductionist biases in his treatment of the communal question which led him, in practice, to underplay the role of political-ideological struggle against communalism". He said so in a lecture under the same title but of much larger size.[13]

The first was more important as it covers everybody. There is nothing in the five volumes of the *Letters to Chief Ministers* Nehru wrote as the Prime Minister, which suggests that he is interested in raising and depending on a mass movement to back up some of his policies to be executed from above.

Similarly, Economist V.K.R.V. Rao wrote "The common man…did not get any significant benefit as a result of the Five-Year Plans."[14] Therefore, Nehru had in the main nothing but the bureaucracy to depend upon to go ahead with his policies, domestic or foreign. Rao said that "In no democratic country in the world do we find the offices of Governors and Ministers functioning in such isolation and lack of mass contact or identification as we find in independent India."[15] Here we are reminded of Gandhi's advice in his "An Indian Governor" on how the Indian Governors, a new phenomenon at the time of independence to take the place of the British ones, to behave.[16] There was probably some continuity from the British Raj. There was, of course, the Parliament which Nehru highly respected. But did Nehru relate himself to the masses? In this connection Nehru's letter of 9 June, 1951 to Rajaji was significant. He writes that "Throughout my public life, I have drawn my strength chiefly from my contacts with the people. Those contacts grow less and less…We rely more and more on official agencies which are generally fairly good, but which are completely different in outlook and execution from anything that draws popular enthusiasm to it."[17]

On the second point by Bipan Chandra, here is an example. In an article first printed in the *Foreign Affairs* in 1938, Nehru said that "There is no religious or communal problem in India. What is called the religious or communal problem is really a dispute among upper class people for a division of the spoils of office or of representation in a legislature." What is there is "But the real problems of India…are economic…The land problem is the outstanding question of India and without revolutionary changes in our agriculture and land system it is difficult to see any final solution of it."[18] Nehru may be correct. But did he not put a fullstop to the issue only by reaching the above conclusion, without asking how to bring about changes in agriculture and land system in a more concrete way? The result is that the communal problem itself is left beyond serious consideration.

Foreign Policy

Tenth, on Nehru's foreign policy, we will again see what Rao writes.[19] He says that "the one thing Gandhi succeeded in stamping upon Nehru was the method of attaining peace, that peace has to be fought for and won, and that there are peaceful methods for winning peace." Nehru fought for peace by his non-alignment policy, and, as Rao says, it has prevented the Third World War from actually breaking out.[20] So far at least he was right, although there are different views as to if India is still a non-aligned country or not at this time. Katherine Frank, for example, writes in her *Indira,* a biography of Indira Gandhi, that, in the course of the negotiations on the "Treaty of Peace, Friendship and Cooperation" with the Soviet Union in 1971, "Haksar (the then Prime Minister's Principal Private Secretary) also added a clause restating India's commitment to non-alignment, though ironically, the pact served to bury this Nehruvian principle once and for all."[21]

More importantly, it is doubtful if Nehru always fought for peace by peaceful methods. The war India fought with China could certainly have been averted by Nehru himself as we will see in the following pages. One interesting comment on non-alignment, by the way, is what John W. Garver writes in his *Protracted Contest: Sino-Indian Rivalry in the Twentieth Century*. Basing his argument on Peter Willetts' *The Non-Aligned Movement: The Origin of a Third World Alliance*, he says on the "Brioni Communique" of 1956, sponsored by the then Yugoslavia's President Tito, that it was no doubt a statement for the benefits of those countries that do not join either of the two camps, but what was unique about India is that she has not adopted non-alignment as a policy for her defence.[22]

Notes

1. Yamaguchi, *How Relevant is Gandhi Today*, 79.
2. Nehru, *An Autobiography*, 527-533.
3. Iyengar, Uma and L. Zackariah, *Together They Fought*, 390.

4. Yamaguchi, *How Relevant is Gandhi Today*, 19.
5. *Ibid.*, 138-9.
6. *Ibid.*, 54.
7. *Ibid.*, 179-183.
8. *Ibid.*, 49.
9. Nehru, *An Autobiography*, 264, 273, 281.
10. Yamaguchi, *How Relevant is Gandhi Today*, 96.
11. *Ibid.*, 132.
12. Bipan Chandra, Mridula and Aditya Mukherjee, *India Since Independence*, 230-2.
13. Bipan Chandra, *The Writings of Bipan Chandra*, 134-5.
14. Rao, V.K.R.V., *The Nehru Legacy*, 50.
15. *Ibid.*, 18.
16. Yamaguchi, *How Relevant is Gandhi Today*, 67.
17. Nehru, *The Essential Writings of Jawaharlal Nehru*, Vol. II, 728.
18. *Ibid.*, Vol. I, 38-9.
19. Yamaguchi, *How Relevant is Gandhi Today*, 223.
20. Rao, V.K.R.V., *The Nehru Legacy*, 36.
21. Frank, Katherine, *Indira*, 334.
22. Garver, J.W., *Protracted Contest*, 121.

3
Analysis by Dipak Malik in *Gandhi aur Nehru*

Gandhi from Among the People

In the previous chapter we have seen how Nehru's thought has been influenced by, or interacted with, that of Gandhi. Here we will further pursue the question by examining a recent work right on the subject, Dipak Malik's *Gandhi aur Nehru*. The book is in Hindi.

It says in the Preface that the collaboration of the two men leading to their "*aam sahamati* (general cooperation)" made the foundation of modern India, and the book wants to throw light again on their cooperation and work. It also says that they will ignore those people who use their whole capital to try to show the difference between the two as if it really existed which in fact did not. Some of the relevant points of Malik's analysis concerning the above objective are as follows:

(1) Gandhi did not land on this earth by parachute, but emerged from among the people with the message of *abhaya*[1] (fearlessness). This is very much like what Nehru says in the *Discovery of India,* which is "And then Gandhi came...He did not descend from the top; he seemed to emerge from the millions of India, speaking their language and incessantly drawing attention to them and their appalling condition...The essence of his teaching was fearlessness and truth...."[2] P.C. Joshi also says in his *Mahatma Gandhi: The New Economic Agenda* that Gandhi was "a new type of social thinker and political leader who had emerged on the Indian scene through a long process of trial and testing by the masses themselves."[3] Gandhi and Nehru between them became the chief craftsmen in the work of India's independence.

Emergence of Communalism

(2) In the year Gandhi arrived in Durban, 1893, the Hindu-Muslim relations were the worst in India. Gandhi's African experience impressed him with the significance of Hindu-Muslim relations. The Muslim middle classes were troubled by a number of issues such as sacred cow, municipal elections, the common language.[4] The influence of Mazzini of Italy was great on Gandhi. His Italy was that of labourers and peasants. In Gandhi's view, Nehru was the *nayak* (leader) of the Indian unification.

(3) It was not possible for the two to fight the freedom movement without touching the Hindu-Muslim relations. This characterization of Nehru would rather go against the second point raised by Bipan Chandra mentioned in the previous Chapter. Anyway, the leaders of the majority like Tilak, Banerjea, Ghosh and Rai looked at the problem to be out of the agenda.[5] The rise of communalism on both sides coincided with the rise of the respective new classes.[6]

(4) The movement for the protection of the sacred cow amounted to the destruction by the Hindus of the Hindu-Muslim solidarity at the time of 1857. Malik has introduced a very fresh topic of the life of Munshi Rahman Khan, a Pathan from Bundelkhand, who has gone to Surinam in South America and tried to build a composite culture there at the beginning of the twentieth century. Khan's diary shows a very unique experience in mixing cultures. The common language was Hindustani. However, the arrival of Arya Samaj in Surinam has also brought communalism with it. Swami Dayananda formed the first cow protection organization in the Punjab in 1882, and the growth of these organizations contributed a great deal to the expansion of the Congress in Uttar Pradesh in the early stages. The educated Muslims identified the Congress in Uttar Pradesh with the cow protection movement.[7] Arya Samaj, the Muslim Press and the Muslim League were greatly responsible for the growth of communalism in the Punjab.[8] On the other hand there was no communalism in the reform movement of Brahmo Samaj or of Vivekananda in Bengal.

(5) It did not seem meaningful to the two to fight elections under the limited franchise, although Gandhi gradually came to realize the significance of the in-House struggle, and called India "the largest and fullest democracy known to the world" even under the 1935 Government of India Act.

(6) The various indicators of communalism since 1893 were to be seen in the Morley-Minto reforms. When Gandhi returned to India, he thought the Hindu-Muslim question was the first to take on. But he had never experienced it before. The first time he saw the attempt to fight it was the Lucknow Pact of 1916. But, the Pact reached only a handful of people. The Khilafat gave him an opportunity. In order to have a bridge with the masses, Gandhi connected it to the No Cooperation Movement, instead of depending on the priest class, to make it an inclusive nationalism.[9] Malik says "*sajha*" to refer to the cooperation of the two people in Hindu-Muslim relations, the caste system, the untouchables question and the economic issues.[10]

Nationalism in the Middle East and India

(7) Nehru took a more class-oriented approach and did not look at the Muslim League as the representative of the Indian Muslims. This is more in tune with Bipan Chandra's comment. His religious neutrality originated from this time. He found new nationalism in Kemal Ataturk of Turkey. His view of the Khilafat in *the Discovery of India* was different from Gandhi's. M.A. Ansari or Maulana Azad welcomed the movements in Turkey, Egypt and Iran. This was a new trend in Indian Muslim nationalism.[11] How was it to be related to the support to the Palestinian nationalism? Gandhi was indifferent to Kemal. But the two cooperated. To Gandhi the greatest problem was that of unity based on religious equality. For Nehru it was that of religion-neutral democracy. Both stressed the protection of the minorities.[12]

Provincial Coalition and Muslim Mass Contact

(8) Many historians have sought the origin of Pakistan in the Congress refusal to form provincial coalition Governments with the League in 1937. But the main enemy of the Congress at the time was the Agriculturalist Party which was the landlords' party, and the League also fought it. The League was not fighting the Congress. Therefore, it was natural for the League to expect some seats in the Governments after the elections.[13] It was then thought that if the majority of the Hindu votes could be obtained, similarly, it would be possible to get votes for the Congress from among the Muslims.

(9) The League represented both communalism and the interests of the *Zamindars*. It would be immature, however, to conclude that therefore, Nehru did not place confidence in achieving communal unity through the League. He tried to have contacts with the Muslim masses.

(10) The mass contact movement was launched by Ashraf and other Muslim intellectuals on 31 March, 1937.[14] The right wing of the Congress and the Hindu Mahasabha were against the mass contact and socialism, afraid of this new movement turning a second Khilafat. Anyway, it did not reach the Muslim kisans,[15] and was wound up in 1939. It was killed by Pant, Kripalani, and Morarji Desai.[16] Ironically, therefore, the right wing in the Congress thus freed the League from a great offensive which could have successfully opposed the two-nation theory.[17] Judith Brown writes on Nehru at this time that "Despite his deep concern at the failure of Congress to attract Muslim voters, his personal failure of vision at this stage was to underestimate the power of what he dismissed as communalism."[18] This criticism is in tune with that of Bipan Chandra.

(11) The peace in the twentieth century and the avoidance of the Third World War were due to Nehru and the Non-aligned Movement.[19] This is what Rao says also, as we saw before. Malik's narrative here, however, jumped from the failure of the mass contact movement in Uttar Pradesh to Nehru's post-independence foreign policy.

(12) Malik concludes that Nehruvian *Arm Sahamati* and *Sarvadharmasambhava* (tolerance to all religions) have long been in India's cultural tradition, which the two have spread widely. Gandhi interpreted religion according to the requirements of the age. He was the greatest traveller in that way.[20]

The author interviewed Dipak Malik in February 2016 after the book was out. Malik told him that he was in a minority in the sense that not many would agree that the distance between the two diminished, instead of widening, with the passage of time. He also said that the Hindu-Muslim relations were the most important as the basic framework of the newly independent state, but so far Gandhi's view and Nehru's view on this point had been studied separately from each other, and not in interaction.

In this work that deficiency had been taken on beautifully. The book, however, discusses it practically only up to independence and no more. So, its second volume is to be waited for. Also the references to Nehru's writings are not as many as one may expect, less than a dozen times altogether, and they are mostly from *The Discovery* and *An Autobiography*.

Notes

1. Malik, Dipak, *Gandhi aur Nehru*, 12.
2. Nehru, *The Discovery of India*, 392-3.
3. Yamaguchi, *How Relevant is Gandhi Today*, 68-9.
4. Malik, Dipak, *Gandhi aur Nehru*, 27.
5. *Ibid.*, 35-6.
6. *Ibid.*
7. *Ibid.*, 57.
8. *Ibid.*, 47.
9. *Ibid.*, 72.
10. *Ibid.*, 17-8.
11. *Ibid.*, 75.
12. *Ibid.*, 82.
13. *Ibid.*, 86-7.
14. *Ibid.*, 97.
15. *Ibid.*, 103.
16. *Ibid.*, 102.
17. *Ibid.*, 105.
18. Brown, Judith, *Nehru*, 60.
19. Malik, Dipak, *Gandhi aur Nehru*, 132.
20. *Ibid.*, 176.

4
Nehru's Economics

Toward a Socialist Economy by Planning

Then we will look at some of the basic economic thinking which was at the base of the socio-economic policies of Nehru as the Prime Minister. We will pick it up from Nehru's *Letters to Chief Ministers 1947-1964* (LCM), edited by G. Parthasarathi, the 5-volume collection of letters he, as the Prime Minister, wrote to the Chief Ministers of the States over the 18 years he presided over the all-India politics. These volumes contain nearly 400 letters in almost 3,000 pages put together. The letters were supposed to have been written on the fortnightly basis, but that understanding was not always followed. The first one was written on 15 October, 1947, exactly two months after India achieved independence. The one written on 21 May, 1963 was practically the last letter contained here. After that, during the last year of his life, he wrote only one very short note on 21 December, 1963. At any rate there is nothing else contained in those volumes from this last year. Even in that note he says nothing to explain what had happened to his letter-writing programme.

It was a little more than two years after independence that Nehru for the first time made clear his interest in planning. He said, "I think that the time has come when we should take some step towards the development of a suitable planning authority" (LCM, 1-472). It is rather ironical that this was written on the *Gandhi Jayanti*, 1949, as Gandhi was very critical of the National Planning Committee of the Congress of which Nehru was the Chairman before the Second World War. This time also Nehru as the Prime Minister became the Chairman of the Planning Commission that came into being as the result of his proposal. Probably, he wanted to associate the name of Gandhi with the Planning Commission, or more broadly with the concept of planning.

Then on 3 March, 1952 he inaugurated the Institute of Technology at Kharagpur, the first of the celebrated group of IITs which were indispensable to his concept of planning (LCM, 2-571). Some time later he used a phrase in one of his letters, which was going to be often quoted. He said on the purpose of planning that "I take it that our objective is to have ultimately a socialist economy. I am not using the word in any doctrinaire sense, but in its broad meaning" (LCM, 4-45).

It was going to be "a mixed economy", but "with the progressive growth of the public sector", and therefore "a socialist pattern" (LCM, 4-100). There was a Lok Sabha resolution (LCM, 4-112), and the Avadi resolution by the Congress Session along these lines. For that sort of socialism Nehru emphasized that "Whatever the shape of planning in the future, it is admitted now that the production of power and of steel are essential bases for it (LCM, 4-122). P.C. Mahalanobis, as the Statistical Adviser to the Government of India, produced his famous "Plan Frame" for the Second Five-Year Plan, and there was a Panel of Economists in the Planning Commission (LCM, 4-178). Nehru himself was of the view that "on the whole we aim at a decentralized economy" (LCM, 4-189).

There is an interesting expression in his narrative of Europe, this time of Italy toward the end of 1955. He wrote of the "vast sums of money" the US had given to that country in aid, and said that "But the condition of the peasantry, especially in South Italy, is deplorable. Hardly any part of the aid has trickled down to the masses of the people" (LCM, 4-306-7). Was he familiar with the trickle-down theory, and its defects?

There was a New Industrial Policy of 1956 and the Second Plan as an embodiment of it. As regards the position of the two segments in the plan he said that they are "allowing private enterprise to develop in the secondary fields, which are not of strategic importance. Gradually, the public sector will grow both absolutely and relatively, and the whole economy of the country will be controlled by it" (LCM, 4-460-1). So, this is the essence of his socialism, namely the hegemony of the public sector in the economy.

Between the Large and the Small

As for the position of the big and small sectors in the economy, he had some interesting things to say. "We have paid a great deal of attention to huge schemes of development in a number of river valleys and for industries like iron and steel, fertilizers etc. These were essential. At the same time, I feel more and more that we should concentrate in future on small schemes spread out all over the country. This fact impressed itself upon me in Japan" (LCM, 4-597-8). He had just returned from Japan.

There was then the Ooty (Ootacamund) Seminar in the middle of 1959. Around this time Nehru seemed to be optimistic about the future of the Indian economy. For example, he talked about the family planning in this way. "As you know, I am all for family planning and birth control and an attempt to reduce the rate of population growth in India, but I am convinced that whatever the population growth, our food production can increase more rapidly." He mentioned the possibility of stepping up the per acre yield and of bringing vast areas under cultivation (LCM, 5-257). At the beginning of 1960 Nehru was hopeful that "we may approach a stage of a large measure of self-sufficiency and an economy which is self-generating" (LCM, 5-353). On the possibility of mechanization in agriculture, Nehru said that "It is only when our growing industry absorbs a large number of the people who depend on agriculture now that we can think in terms of progressive mechanization" (LCM, 5-354). It was still much too early to think of mechanization in agriculture, but Nehru, whether it was a dream or not, was able to expand his imagination to that subject.

Talking of the socialistic pattern, he said in mid-1961, which was at the beginning of the Third Plan, that "Probably it can only be at the beginning of the Fifth Plan that India can think with some satisfaction of its achievements leading to a self-generating economy and a higher level of living standards. It will be then that the socialist pattern of society, which we aim at, will take shape" (LCM, 5-437). At this time, the Third Plan itself was not yet complete and Nehru was expecting the report on the plan would be published soon. So, he said, "Our *panchayats*...should consider it and discuss it and indeed criticize it where needed. Our schools and colleges should also discuss it; our trade unions and other organizations should do likewise. Only thus can we get a nationwide appreciation of what we are aiming at, what we have already done, and what we intend to achieve, not only in the five years to come, but also subsequently" (*Ibid.*).

This "discussion", as he called it, was going to replace the mass movement when there was no NC, CD, or the Quit India of 1942. This was the crucial difference from Gandhi and this is what Bipan Chandra pointed out. But, this is as much as Nehru could have done. Having understood his defects in placing himself in connection from the masses, he wanted to do as much as he could do. Suppose there was no China War of 1962, for example, would he have done it, to a considerable extent? Anyhow, he could not and would not dismount, as we will see.

Social Sector

In the social sector Nehru paid more attention to "education and health" (LCM, 5-89) than others. But, it is not clear which part of education, primary, secondary or higher, was to be stressed in his thought. Similarly, what stage of public health, primary care or referral, or any specific diseases to be targeted on a nation-wide scale or other specific objectives to be promoted is not clear, though "the eradication of smallpox" is mentioned in one of the letters (LCM, 5-497). There is no mention of safe drinking water with all what it implies.

Nehru said of "the great objectives that we have" that "There must be a life worthwhile for all the hundreds of millions who live here so that all of us can lead a purposeful existence and rid ourselves of the curses of poverty, unemployment, disease and ignorance" (LCM, 5-601). He continued, "In the final analysis, right education open to all is perhaps the basic remedy for most of our ills." This education must be "to a large extent" technical training, it must be cultural and spiritual, but "It must essentially be mass education" (*Ibid.*). These are from his letter of 21 May, 1963, practically his last as has been indicated in the above. Therefore, we may well take it his very last message. But, why is it that even at this stage the mass education is 'perhaps' the basic remedy?

Food and Agriculture

We will select some of the areas of economic activities and see how Nehru tried to tackle them.

Even before Nehru turned to his favourite planning, he got himself busy with the various measures for stepping up the food production. The Food Grains Committee suggested in 1947 "greater attention to be paid to minor irrigation, local manure, distribution of improved seeds, reclamation of land and setting up of village panchayats and cooperatives so that the targets in food production could be achieved" (LCM, 1-38fn7). Those items overlap the interests of Nehru himself. He wrote that "I suggest to you to lay stress on the use of compost" (LCM, 1-427), or "minor irrigation works are to be pushed" (LCM, 1-441), or "the real way to increase our food production is by increasing the yield from the land that is already cultivated" (LCM, 2-212). What is interesting in this connection is that Nehru seemed to think that "the average yield is far greater in China than in India" (LCM, 4-429).

On the other hand he also writes that "We are in fact much more advanced industrially and in regard to communications than China. I was told the other day by a recent Indian visitor to China, who is a good observer, that it will take about ten to fifteen years for China to come up to the present level of India's development" (LCM, 3-401). This was in October 1953. It was only four years since the Chinese Revolution, China's development had been very lopsided geographically and otherwise, and it is possible to judge that China's standard was not up to that of India at least on certain points. One wonders, however, if Nehru had not drawn a conclusion from this observation that China's military level was also inferior to India and the idea had not lingered till 1962.

Nehru also shows interest in "compost and manures and the like" rather than chemical fertilizers (LCM, 4-394, 5-251-2). This may be a legacy of Gandhi. He also points out that "Take the plough. A simple modern plough can obviously do much greater work than the old one which just scratches the surface of the soil" (LCM, 5-354). He lists the following four items as "the heart of the matter in regard to progress in agriculture", namely better seeds, better implements and ploughs, green manure, and small irrigation works (*Ibid.*, 406). Cultivation should not be expanded at the expense of the forests (LCM, 4-442, 602). Even on the goat he said that "A goat is more dangerous for crops or anything that grows in the field or garden than any other animal...Instead of goats, attempts may be made to keep sheep" (LCM, 4-610).

The following table shows the movement of the average per capita availability of food grains (cereals and pulses, in grams per day) from 1951 to 1966, effectively during the Nehru era. Each year is the agricultural year (July to June). The figures are by the Ministry of Agriculture, and were published in *Statistical Pocket Book 1971* by the Central Statistical Organisation of the Government of India (Table 21, partial).

Year	*Cereals*	*Pulses*	*Food grains (Cereals and Pulses)*
1951	334	61	395
1956	366	71	431
1961	399	69	468
1966P	356	48	404

One would immediately notice the great fluctuation over the years in the average availability of food grains, which is a very large minus factor in judging the standard of living of a people.

River Valley Development

Nehru was from the beginning keenly interested in the river valley development schemes, especially those on a large scale. Damodar (LCM, 1-71-2), Mahanadi (*Ibid.*, 101), Bhakra-Nangal (LCM, 2-587), Tungabhadra (LCM, 3-114) were some of the early examples of his interest. When legislation for the Authority for the Damodar Valley was passed, he even wrote on 20 February, 1948 that "I consider this in many ways to be the most notable piece of legislation that has ever been passed in this country" (LCM, 1-71-2). He wanted to spread these large-scale projects to the whole country. He wrote, "We must take up our major development schemes before very long, because on them depends the future progress of the country" (*Ibid.*, 473). Or, "By laying the foundations of large-scale scientific work, we have done something which is of essential importance for the future of India" (LCM, 2-326). He further visited Damodar (LCM, 3-251, 4-285), and Bhakra-Nangal, which is "a tremendous affair" (LCM, 3-434). And he reported on "the inauguration of the Bhakra-Nangal canal system" soon afterwards (*Ibid.*, 605).

As far as the letters in those volumes are concerned, it is doubtful if Nehru reconsidered the value of those large-scale projects from the point of view of the possible damages they would give to the environmental conditions, or of the resettlement of the inhabitants and the livestock that would be affected by those projects. It is true that he also pays attention to "undertaking relatively small schemes" (LCM, 1-293). But, it is because of efficiency and 'rapid results', and it is doubtful if he had environmental or human consideration in mind as well.

Some years later, when he was able to extricate himself from the talks on Indo-Chinese conflict, Nehru went to a place called Navagam and inaugurated the vast Narmada River Valley Project. It was on 5 April, 1961. It was one of the pillars of India's basic infrastructural programmes. It was estimated that the Narmada River system, which flows westward into the Arabian Sea, was the least developed among India's major river systems. He called it one of the "temples of modern India" like he had called some other river projects in the same way (SWJN-2, 68-32-3). But, before long it became clear that this huge project would generate environmental problem and rehabilitation and resettlement problem for tens of thousands of population. Nehru passed away without knowing them.

Back in early 1958 Nehru was happy to write that an American expert of soil conservation told the press in India that "if proper soil conservation practices were applied to land in India, production could be increased three to four times to solve the food problem of the country" (LCM, 5-5).

On the other hand he was troubled by the drought that he saw in his own district of Allahabad in Uttar Pradesh in the middle of the same year. He wrote, "This district had been hard hit because of drought for almost three years running. To a small extent, it is irrigated. Large numbers of peasants complained to me about their difficulties in obtaining water from the canals or the water channels. They complained of the petty employees of the Irrigation Department who harassed them or wanted money from them" (*Ibid.*, 5-108). On the whole, "What is necessary is intensive cultivation by better irrigation facilities, better seeds and manures and fertilizers" (*Ibid.*).

Nehru who has "become enamoured of big projects" wrote that "what seems to me much more necessary are the small projects, the minor irrigation facilities" and calls attention to the fact that "in South India particularly a vast number of tanks have gone into disrepair." He adds something very interesting. "The *zamindar* in the old days looked after them (tanks). Since the disappearance of the *zamindari* system no one else appears to have been made responsible for them" (*Ibid.*, 5-138).

May be a word here also on Nehru's interest in land relations.

Nehru shows much interest in the land relation even after the abolition of the *Zamindari* system. He says that "The next step appears to be some kind of redistribution of land so as to put an end to large holdings," but also says that 25 acres as the ceiling line would not be enough to produce enough surplus land to be distributed to the landless. He continues that "We could help the landless more by developing uncultivated land" (LCM, 3-37-8). If the productivity of land goes up 25 acres will turn out to be too high. On the other hand was he sure that there was enough uncultivated land left to be distributed?

In September 1957 Nehru wrote that "I have recently been to Mysore to attend the Gramdan Conference convened by the Sarva Seva Sangha at the instance of Acharya Vinoba Bhave" (LCM, 4-562, also see the following[1]). The Government had to depend on the *Bhoodan* Movement to have more surplus land to distribute among the landless. By this time the newly installed Communist State Government in Kerala also was submitting their own alternative for land reform.

Note

1. Yamaguchi, *How Relevant is Gandhi Today*, 144.

5
Poverty and Development in Longer Perspective as seen by Dreze and Sen

Dreze and Sen's Work

The problem of poverty which was left unsolved in the Nehru era, and which may have increased in its intensity at least in certain dimensions, has been most systematically discussed in a recent book *An Uncertain Glory: India and Its Contradictions*, 2013, co-authored by Jean Dreze and Amartya Sen. This is the latest in the series of works on the Poverty of India by these two scholars which started with *India: Economic Development and Social Opportunity*, 1995. We will borrow some of the indices of poverty in India from this work, and will try to place the Nehru era in a longer perspective. They are from the Japanese translation and therefore, we do not mention pages here from the original work.

[According to the two authors, in India even now one in every three of the population has no access to electricity, while in China the ratio is only 1 per cent.] If you look at the general economic growth, it was not remarkable in India from 1950s to 1970s, which covers the entire Nehru era and more. Interestingly, the authors say that it is as difficult to prove that Nehru tried to bring socialism to India as to prove that the economy stagnated because of the economic planning in his era.

A Bangalore Seminar

Here we will divert our attention a little from the two scholars and quote a few points from a report of a seminar attended by a number of eminent persons held in (the then) Bangalore in commemoration of Nehru's birth centenary about thirty years ago. Sukhamoy Chakravarty said in his keynote address that he was unable to accept that the 'textile first' strategy would have been superior to Nehru's heavy industry-oriented one. But he agreed that "agriculture was somewhat neglected". P.R. Brahmananda, however, "argued that from the point of 'well-being of the people' Nehru's contribution to development was minimal." Also, "a point reiterated by many was that much of what was expected did not happen mainly because Nehru made many political compromises, and relied heavily upon the essentially colonial administrative system for plan implementation." The report continued to say that "It was also pointed out by some participants that during Nehru period no conscious effort was made to formulate poverty-focused development strategy despite loud talk of socialism."[1]

In his previous book the author tried to show the prevailing poverty in rural India with the help of two tables on Operational Holdings, particularly showing the sharp decline in the Average Area Operated per Holding, and the general impoverishment in the agricultural sector, both during the Nehru era and beyond, or much beyond. In fact, the so-called "Hindu rate of growth" prevailed till the mid-1970s. The table on the Per Capita Availability of Food Grains shown in the last chapter would be in tune with these figures although the coverage was limited time-wise to the Nehru era.

Hirashima Shigemochi and his team have found that "the existing literature on inclusive growth (in India) is overwhelmingly concentrated on the trend and extent of inequality", covering both "increasing interstate disparity" and "widening intrastate disparity". It is inferred also that the land price is rising "beyond what is affordable for the landless and marginal households."[2] One interesting finding here is the close connection of caste and class in the State of Bihar. The lower you are placed in the caste hierarchy, the less the size of the average land holding, and the greater the proportion of the landless households tend to be. The distinction of the Upper OBCs and the Lower OBCs is the crucial dividing line in this combined caste-class hierarchy. The Muslims find themselves above the Scheduled Castes and below the Lower OBCs.[3]

Social Sector

If we go back to Dreze and Sen with these additional points of view and try to get some more material on India's poverty, we will find ourselves amply rewarded particularly in the areas of public health and education till today. Their work pays special attention, for instance, to the level of nutrition of children. In South Asia including India the ratio of underweight children is high. In Africa south of the Sahara the ratio is 25 per cent. But in South Asia it is over 40 per cent. It is still higher in India.

According to Dreze and Sen, in the field of public health the shortage of vaccine for children is a particularly grave problem. The death from measles alone exceeds more than 1,00,000 a year which is nearly half of the figure for the world total. There is a great inter-State difference in the activities of the Primary Health Centres in India. They are very active in some States, but in some others they are almost as good as closed as there is hardly any attendance of the staff there. One point in connection with the underweight children in India is that the increase in the weight of the Indian women during their pregnancy is only 5 kg. This is half the figure for Africa. The BMI (body mass index) is less than 18.5 for 36 per cent of the adult women in India, while the corresponding figure for Africa is 14 per cent.

We will take a more recent figure for vaccination from Jo McGowan Chopra's article in the *Wire* titled "India Leads in Vaccine Production but Not in Vaccination" on 30 April, 2018. It says that "only 18 per cent of India's children receive the full three-dose course of the vaccine against diphtheria, pertussis and tetanus (DPT), and only a third get the measles vaccine by the recommended age of 10 months."

In his previous book the author discussed the reasons given by G. Balatchandirane on why the higher education in independent India got more resources than perhaps it deserved at the time.[4] Here, we will look at some interesting figures showing one aspect of India's higher education 70 years after independence. In an article "Why

Are There Still Such Few SCs, STs and OBCs at IIMs?" on the *Wire* of 18 January, 2018, Siddharth Joshi and Deepak Malghan, themselves members of an IIM faculty, write that among the 642 faculty members of the 13 IIMs, including the 7 established in this century, only 4 belong to the Scheduled Castes, 1 to the Scheduled Tribes, and 17 to the OBCs. In contrast to Balatchandirane's—if we may say so-quantitative analysis, this is a qualitative observation showing why the socio-economic characteristic of India's higher education is not able to change but tends to persist.

We will borrow one more point from Dreze and Sen on the education in India. The children are supposed to go to schools for about 200 days every school year. In reality, however, classes are given for only about 50 days. One of the reasons is the high average of the teachers' absences which is about 25 per cent. Under these circumstances the children in India go to school only for 4.4 years on the average. Who was it that emphasized 'mass education'?

Another aspect of Dreze and Sen's analysis of India's poverty is gender inequality. They are repeatedly calling attention to the low and still lowering sex-ratio. They also stress that women's labour participation rate in India is at an extremely low level and shows little sign of improving. Out of 184 countries in the world on which data are available, the number of the countries whose labour participation rate is below India's 29 per cent is only 17. This situation is making it impossible for the women of India to make use of the growing employment opportunities, in sharp contrast to a number of other Asian countries.

More recently, a study has been published by the Thomson Reuters Foundation. According to the study "India is the most dangerous country in the world for women", followed by Afghanistan, Syria, Somalia, and Saudi Arabia (*The Times*, 27 June, 2018). India was ranked fourth in a similar study conducted in 2011. We may add here that India's woman writer Anuradha Roy has told the audience at a recent Hay Festival function in Britain that women are having a very hard time in India.

Notes

1. An EPW team, "Centennial Appraisal of Nehru Legacy; Report on a Seminar", *EPW*, 3 June, 1989. 1212-1216.
2. Hirashima, Oda and Tsujita, eds., *Inclusiveness in India*, 4-6, 65, 92.
3. *Ibid.*, 253.
4. Yamaguchi, *How Relevant is Gandhi Today*, 93-4.

6
Basis of Nehru's Political Behaviour

Nehru's Political Style

Here we will shift our ground from economics to politics and examine the characteristics of Nehru's political style. We will continue to depend heavily on LCM.

A footnote in the LCM says that, in Delhi late in November 1947, three months after independence, "Reaffirming its faith in the secular character and policy of the Congress, the A.I.C.C., called upon the Government to ensure equal rights to all citizens and complete protection to the minorities" (LCM, 1-20fn3). Then in December 1948 the Congress had its Session "after a long interval" at Jaipur (*Ibid.*, 251). It was the first since the War-time Session at Ramgarh in 1940. Actually, it meant that the Congress would not take heed to the advice of Gandhi, who was no more at this time, to dissolve itself into a Lok Sevak Sangh, and would instead continue its existence as a political party, this time onwards a parliamentary party.

On 2 February, 1950, shortly after the first Republic Day, which transformed India from a Dominion to a Republic under its own Constitution, Nehru lamented that "In spite of occasional bursts of enthusiasm among the people, as on the occasion of the celebration of the Republic Day, there is an inertness and passivity and a complete lack of enthusiasm, generally speaking, among the people" (LCM, 2-10). Probably people had expected more to come immediately after independence and their difficulties would have been solved. When Nehru says, however, that "Important developments take place and decisions are taken not in the A.I.C.C., but rather in small groups outside...This itself is significant in indicating that we are cutting ourselves off to some extent from the mass movements and the large scale contacts of the people that have been the backbone of the Congress" (LCM, 2—393-4), what he means to say is not very clear, particularly as it was after the Congress Presidential election when Nehru-backed candidate had been defeated.

But he also said, "Our people should go about the villages and other places explaining the situation and pointing out our difficulties. This personal touch ...goes far. We seem to have lost that touch and very few people go about as they used to in the old days" (LCM, 1-360). Most of the people Nehru was writing to were provincial Congress leaders. Therefore, Nehru was criticising the way the Congress was. He also said that "Our contacts with the masses diminish" (*Ibid.*, 371), or "Perhaps, the most unfortunate development of the past year or two has been the growth of a barrier between governments and the people" (*Ibid.*, 510).

A little later he also wrote that "The only real way of conveying any message to the people is to be in tune with them, to live with them, to speak their language and to understand their ways" (LCM, 3-494). We are reminded of a speech Gandhi made at Patna in 1947 which talked of "to go down to the masses, share their lives, think in their terms and win their confidence."[1] Apparently, Nehru was not there. Is the coincidence a mere accident, or did Nehru study Gandhi's writings and speak his language? We have already seen the critical comment on Nehru's isolation from the masses by Bipan Chandra, and Nehru's own admission of it to Rajaji.

Concerning the administrative system which had been brought over by the British, Nehru said that "The whole structure of the British administration in the past was built up on the district officer" (LCM, 1-420), and "In the main, it was concerned with keeping the peace and collecting taxes. We are trying to use the same structure for economic activities of all kinds, for which it is not suited" (*Ibid.*, 466). And further, "The present system is not especially fitted for urgent disposal of business and we are constantly lost in long notes and repeated references and petty sanctions which delay and obstruct" (LCM, 3—402-3). Concerning the personnel management in the bureaucracy Nehru writes that "It is ...generally desirable for officers not to be kept in a particular post for more than three years at the most" (LCM, 2—215). One wonders if Nehru had a different standard for himself on this point, and if it had got anything to do with having been nominated by Gandhi as his heir, as retirement would seem in his eyes unthinkable. He himself once wrote in "The Rashtrapati" (see the next chapter) that "He must know well that there is no resting by the way in the path he has chosen...for he who rides a tiger cannot dismount" (SWJN-1, 8-520-3).

Development Under Democracy

Then what was Nehru's overall ambition as a politician/statesman, the objective of his domestic policy? On 3 March, 1953, about the time of Stalin's death, Nehru wrote some very important and interesting idea. He said, "More and more it is being realized in other parts of the world that we in India are engaged in a mighty adventure. To build up this country and to solve the problems of poverty and unemployment in a democratic way on this scale is something that has not been done anywhere" (LCM, 3-252). He was right. The social sciences or development studies at his time cannot have reached this standard, of tackling the problems in this way. Neither had the Soviet Union under Stalin which had attracted Nehru in some way but not completely.

If so this was his basic political philosophy. Particularly, that part which emphasizes both economic uplift and democratic way simultaneously was the point which had not attracted the attention of politicians and scholars alike so far. Nehru was very early in reaching this point, and here lies his originality. In Gandhian terms these two may be considered to be the end and the means. Sometimes, afterwards he put it in a more systematic way, thus "But it is untrue, I think, to say that the choice lies between rapid progress with authoritarian methods and a slow advance under democracy" (LCM, 5-179). There are some, particularly among those scholars calling themselves development economists, who say that growth can be generated only by authoritarian methods, and only the growth thus generated will gradually create conditions for political democracy. Such a scenario of development under authoritarianism would go diametrically against Nehru's idea of democratic development mentioned above. The authoritarian development theory would go any further in justifying dictatorial regimes and their undemocratic policies in the name of political theories or modern social sciences. We have seen numerous examples of it in recent years all over the world. So, people like Nehru are, or used to be, in the minority concerning the way how growth and democracy may be brought about together. The struggle is still being fought between the two ways of development.

In order for these two to be brought together, the minimum should be provided for the masses in a tangible way so that they may take active interest in the development process, participate in it and offer cooperation. In his previous book the author mentioned that, borrowing from Arjun Sengupta and others, some of the most important items that constitute development in this sense would be "education, safe drinking water, prevention of diseases, protection of forestry and soil, organic fertilizer, and irrigation depending upon the availability of water", and called it an alternative path of development, as these are not usually placed at the centre of the picture. These may also be broadly called as the Basic Human Needs which will constitute the inescapable condition of poverty alleviation of our time.[2] The vast underprivileged people may not be able to have access to them on their own. Did Nehru, while conscious of the difference between the various ways of development, pay sufficient attention to these needs while he was in a position to take them up? It is difficult for us to answer in the affirmative, as there is not much to show that there was a dialogue with the masses on these points. This is why he was not able to find what to do in the rather unlikely event of early retirement, as he confessed to his sister Vijayalakshmi Pandit (*see* chapter 8).

Nehru and the Socialists

We will also look at Nehru's relations with the Socialists, or the Congress Socialist Party (hereafter CSP) as they called themselves up to independence. R.N.P. Singh's *Nehru A Troubled Legacy* contains as Appendix 22 Nehru's letter to Rajendra Prasad, the President of the Constituent Assembly, of 5 July, 1947, shortly before partition. Enclosure 1 of this Appendix is a copy of JP's reply to Nehru on 3 May which says "if invited" he would recommend "Deva (Narendra), Aruna (Asaf Ali), Lohia (Ram Manohar), Purushottam Trikamdas,

Kamaladevi (Chattopadhyay), Rao Patwardhan, Asoka Mehta, and if coming home Achyut Patwardhan.[3] JP's own name is not there. This was the decision of the National Executive of the CSP. Nehru replied on 5 July, the copy of which is there as Enclosure 2, that he would welcome, but it would depend on vacancies.[4]

Apparently, Nehru invited JP to recommend some Socialist names who could be accommodated into the first Cabinet of independent India. He had had three socialists among the members of the Congress Working Committee when he was elected President in 1936. From his reply, however, Nehru did not seem to be very serious in enlisting the cooperation of the Socialists at this time. This was the time when Patel was still there. It seems he was having his own dialogue with JP as is shown elsewhere in this book. Did Nehru at all confer with him on the possibility of having some socialists in the Cabinet? Not very likely.

After several years the two were again discussing the same subject, and Appendix 23 of Singh's book is a copy of JP's reply to Nehru dated 4 March, 1953. JP writes, "I do not find today Gandhiji's dynamism and incessant quest towards his ultimate values except in Vinoba...". JP says that "integrated and far-reaching agrarian reform...the most urgent reform that is needed" should be included in the programme before discussing the possible names of Ministers, and they, therefore, made such a draft programme. JP further says, "This in brief, is my conception of the purposes and possibilities of our cooperation. If it be not also yours, I should respectfully urge that the whole idea be dropped." Apparently, JP was less keen on obtaining offices either for him or his colleagues than on putting some of his programmes into practice.

JP's Draft Programme consists of 14 items in seven sections. As was mentioned, the author listed six items in his previous book, apart from the land and the accompanying employment problem, as the necessary elements in any alternative development thinking. He is not able to find any of them in the JP's Programme.

Nehru's Legacies and Kerala

What is left behind as Nehru's legacies? It seems there are two, parliamentary democracy and equal treatment of all religions. Judith

Brown writes that "He treated the Lok Sabha in Delhi with utmost seriousness...."[5] Vincent Sheean also says that nobody would pay so much respect to the Parliament and its activities.[6] S. Gopal says in his biography of Nehru that "democracy in India—adult suffrage, a sovereign Parliament, a free press, an independent judiciary—is Nehru's most lasting monument...it was perhaps the only way of holding India together."[7] As if to reciprocate Nehru's respect to the Parliament, only one no confidence motion had been presented during the whole of the Nehru era, which was on the war with China.[8] K.V. Kesavan has told the author not only once that as a young scholar he used to go to the Lok Sabha to listen to the debate going on there, and he mentioned a number of the first-rank debaters at the time who had charmed him with their oratory.

Then how do we explain what happened in Kerala under Nehru? Did he not dismiss a democratically elected State Government there? Yes, he did. Kerala was one of the new south Indian States born in 1956 in accordance with the linguistic States policy. In the *LCM* Nehru discusses it on 2 July, 1959 for the first time. It was after making a short trip to that State, where he found that "Kerala is divided into two solid groups, those opposing and those supporting the Kerala State Government" (LCM, 5-271). It was rather the Communist State Government that showed interest in Nehru's mediation than the Opposition including the Congress, but Nehru's conclusion was that "In the circumstances, I felt that the only peaceful way out of this deadlock was to have general elections in the State" (*Ibid.*, 272), meaning the dismissal of the State Government under that name, a decision backed up by the Congress leadership with his daughter as its current President. On the last day of that month the Legislative Assembly of Kerala was dissolved and the State Government was taken over by the Central Government.

Here, we will examine what is contained in the SWJN-2 on the situation in Kerala at this time. It was in the above atmosphere that the AICC unanimously adopted the resolution "The Situation in Kerala" in October 1958, saying "The AICC is concerned at...the prevalence of attacks and murderous assaults (on Congressmen and non-Communists) and the policy of the State Government which is often discriminatory and not in accordance of the rule of law" (SWJN, 44-176). It was an attack on the Communist Ministry which had come into existence in April of the previous year 1957 by winning the State elections, headed by Chief Minister E.M.S. Namboodiripad (hereafter E.M.S.). Nehru had written to E.M.S. then that "You can rest assured that not only I but my colleagues have every desire to help" (SWJN, 37-335-8). It must have been a well-meaning letter. On the other hand, E.M.S. and his party formed the Government declaring that they were keen to put into effect those policies the Congress and its Central Government promised the nation but were not able to practice.

There was at least a couple of significant communication from E.M.S. to Nehru before his Government was dismissed at the end of July 1959. One was that in the Kuttanad area big landlords who call themselves Congressmen decided not to lease one and a half lakh acres of land for cultivation that year, which would mean a loss of one lakh of rice production (SWJN, 50, 296-7). They were so much against the Agrarian Relations Bill, which had been moved by the Communist Government in the State Assembly, and this was a strike by the landlords. A number of tenants would be deprived of their employment.

The second was that the anti-Government "Liberation Movement" was supposed to be "completely peaceful and non-violent", and Nehru had said that he would only approve pickets of small number of people, but the reality turned out to be vastly different (SWJN, 50, 302-6). There was no response from the Congress President or the Prime Minister to either of these two.

At the same time, S. Gopal writes that "Nehru's Reaction was Severe" when Nagy of Hungary was executed by the Soviets in June the previous year.[9] Probably, he was confirmed in his conviction that the Communists would decide their policies by directives coming from outside.

Nehru's Defects

At the end of this Chapter we may look at some of the defects in his political behaviour. His aloofness from the masses has been seen before. He was also not good at building consensus by the Cabinet or Cabinet Committees, as we will see in the next chapter. This is related to his likes and dislikes of people which is strong and almost amounts to nepotism. Thus, we are tempted to think that he may have had his sister Vijayalakshmi, the more active of the two sisters, in mind as his possible successor for some time. She had been a Minister in the 1937-39 Uttar Pradesh Congress Government. Look at Nehru's high evaluation of her as a diplomat also in the next chapter.

How did he look at his daughter then? Journalist Kuldip Nayar wrote in *Scoop!*, his memoirs, that Lal Bahadur Shastri, to whom he was very close at that time as Information Officer, had told him that he came to know the successor Nehru had in mind was his daughter. Nayar also tells it in the Preface to his *Between The Lines*. Shastri added that he was not so without an ambition, in other words he was also interested to be Nehru's successor. When U.N. Dhebar's term of office as the Congress President came to an end, Nehru promoted Indira Gandhi and saw to it that she was elected unanimously. The dismissal of the Communist Government in Kerala when she was the Congress President may have to be evaluated with this fact in mind then. Dhebar had succeeded Nehru himself as the Congress President. Maybe Nehru was remembering that he became the Congress President at its Lahore Session in 1929 succeeding his own father who had been its President at its previous Calcutta Session in 1928. Nayar also wrote elsewhere that "Shastri had told me that Nehru wanted Indira to be his successor." There was then the Kamaraj Plan definitely promoting some and handicapping others as Nehru's heir. But Shastri's war-time slogan, "Jai Jawan, Jai Kisan" was so popular, that Indira even told Dinesh Singh, her confidante, that she wanted to retire in the UK. No one had anticipated Shastri's sudden demise at Tashkent.

At the same time, we are somehow forced to the conclusion that Nehru was very tardy in training his fellow politicians and delegating authority to them. We get this impression strongly especially in the field of foreign policy. We will notice that if we look at the composition of the Indian delegation, be it at the Conference on Tibet at Beijing in 1954, or the Bandung Conference the next year (SWJN, 4-159-171), it is predominantly bureaucratic and there are hardly any politicians. We will also see how few, and practically none apart from Krishna Menon, were consulted during the crucial years of Indo-Chinese conflict.

Notes

1. Yamaguchi, *How Relevant is Gandhi Today*, 67.
2. *Ibid.*, 111.
3. Singh, R.N.P., *Nehru*, 301-2.
4. *Ibid.*, 303.
5. Brown, *Nehru*, 105.
6. Sheean, Vincent, *Nehru* (from Japanese translation).
7. Gopal, S., *Jawaharlal Nehru*, Vol. 3, 279.
8. Brown, Judith, *Nehru*, 102.
9. Gopal, S., *Jawaharlal Nehru*, Vol. 3, 60.

7
Nehru-Patel Regime

Nehru and Patel

There has been a great deal of controversy on the relations of the two great men in the early years of independent India, Pandit Jawaharlal Nehru and Sardar Vallabhbhai Patel. People seem to be almost equally divided between the two. We will now study this question of Nehru and Patel mainly by V. Shankar's *My Reminiscences of Sardar Patel*, written by Patel's private secretary and published in two volumes in 1974, and *Inside Story of SardarPatel—The Diary of Maniben Patel: 1936-50*, written by Patel's daughter who had always been with her father and published in 2001. Both of these works have been written from Patel's point of view, but they are not unduly partial. We will also take into consideration Durga Das, ed., *Sardar Patel's Correspondence 1945-1950*, in ten volumes.

What is immediately interesting to the author is that Shankar was a 1931-batch ICS, which was a year when Gandhi, Nehru, Patel and almost everybody were in prison at least part of the year after the Salt March of the previous year. The educated classes of India were divided into two. Or were they two in one? The author was even more surprised that when Shankar was called for an interview for Patel's Private Secretaryship after independence, he was closely interrogated for an hour and a half not only by Patel, his would-be boss, but by two more persons, apparently unqualified, Maniben Patel and G.D. Birla.[1] He was accepted and served in that capacity for four years and three months until Patel's death.

Shankar's father was Motilal Nehru's friend. Patel, we are told, who was then a triumphant leader of the peasant movement at Bardoli,

Gujarat, also was a frequent visitor to the Swaraj Bhavan, Motilal and Jawaharlal's house at Allahabad. On Motilal, the host at this great house, Judith Brown wrote that "It was precisely men like Motilal whom the imperial rulers wished to associate with their government through measures of reform...."[2] He got elected to the provincial legislature for the first time in 1909. But this was all before the emergence of Gandhi, and Motilal changed since then. He was quite instrumental in promoting his only son, Jawaharlal. The way Jawaharlal was promoted by Motilal, particularly in connection with Gandhi, reminds us of the way Indira Gandhi was promoted by her father. We have talked about it already.

Once Motilal requested Patel about his son, "Do take him in your hand; he needs advice and support for he is emotional and apt to run into errors and inconsistencies."[3] Though "Sardar had this request impressed on his mind and heart",[4] Nehru on the other hand did not always try to consult Patel and respect his views, as we will see. But the two were not necessarily on bad terms at all. "Sardar Patel's rise to eminence", writes Durga Das in his Introduction to Volume 2 of *Sardar Patel's Correspondence*, "as a national leader began with his appointment in April 1936 as Chairman of the Congress Parliamentary Board to fight the elections under the Government of India Act of 1935."[5] It is interesting that when Nehru became the Congress President again, Patel became the Chairman of a very important committee of the organization in the same year. This appointment helped to make Patel's grip on the Congress organization incomparably strong.

Until Nehru moved to the present Teen Murti House (Nehru Memorial Museum and Library), probably in July 1948, the two were living nearby, and made a frequent visit to each other, even had a walk together. On this point Maniben writes, perhaps with some nostalgia, "...but this dialogue became very difficult after Nehru moved to the house of the former Commander-in-Chief on Teen Murti Marg. If he had not moved there...much of their later differences might never have developed."[6]

Patel's Style of Work

An episode tells very well how strong Patel's grip on the Congress organization was. On the occasion of the Royal Indian Naval Mutiny early in 1946, even before the arrival of the Cabinet Mission, Nehru who had come to Bombay, presumably to show his support to the Mutiny, gave a press conference on 27 February. One of the questions was "Have you not exhibited indiscipline in the Congress ranks by coming over to Bombay when you were asked by Sardar Vallabhbhai Patel not to do so?" (SWJN-1, 15-15). The author would like to congratulate the Editors of the SWJN-1 for including this question in the series, though the answer is not given.

"Patel never resented advice" was what the then Home Secretary who was British told Shankar. Patel was on very good terms with Socialists, particularly JP and his wife. But when Patel challenged JP and others "to select a province and run it on their socialist principles", they did not respond, presumably because they were not self-confident.[7] If you compare Patel with Nehru, "personal likes and dislikes governed Panditji much more than they did Sardar and were more deep-seated with the former than with the latter."[8] When Patel was ill for six weeks after Gandhi's murder, Nehru did the work of Patel also, and, Shankar writes, "it was a pleasure to work for him…I had felt earlier somewhat nervous about working with him as I had seen him lose his temper with his Private Secretary…more than once. However, I never had that experience during the six weeks that I had the privilege of taking orders from him."[9] We may say Shankar was very fair. Vincent Sheean wrote in his *Nehru: The Years of Power*, not exactly a biography but an observation of Nehru, that he saw his famous bad temper just once during the 12 years of their contact.

Nehru writes about himself in his anonymous article "Rashtrapati" (Congress President in this case, which is what Nehru was at the time), published under the name Chanakya in *the Modern Review* in November 1937, that "His flashes of temper are well known and even when they are controlled, the curling of the lips betrays him."[10] Also see SWJN-1, 2-520-3.

In addition to the Home Ministry, Patel took over the charge of the native Indian States when it was decided that both the new Dominions, India and Pakistan, would have a States Department in July 1947, on the eve of the partition. He established close relations with some Princes like Patiala, Baroda and Bikaner, and some of their Ministers, and through the conversation with them he gradually opened the way for the integration of those States into the Union of India.[11] His work in this field proceeded in two ways, the merger of smaller states with larger ones, starting from the cases of Orissa and Central Province, and the creation of new states like Kathiawad by the union of neighbouring ones, in this case 222 small states. It may be grasped by V.P. Menon's book *The Story of the Integration of Indian States*. V.P. was Secretary in that new Department.

Incidentally, Patel wrote a letter to Chief Ministers dated 3 November, 1949 on behalf of Nehru who had gone on a foreign tour. Patel was the Deputy Prime Minister and four times the Acting Prime Minister on similar occasions. In this letter he wound up his work concerning the Indian States. He wrote, "The month of October has also seen the completion of our integration plans in regard to the States. Although the States concerned, namely, Banaras, Tripura and Manipur are small in size, they are the last to come within the implementation of our integration policy, within the space of less than two years. We have thus completed a great process of unification and democratization."[12]

Jammu & Kashmir

There is one thing we would like to mention here concerning the State of Jammu & Kashmir (hereafter often Kashmir) and Nehru. Kashmir is one of the several major Indian States. It is a common knowledge that out of the 500 strong Indian States, Junagarh, Hyderabad and Kashmir were the three cases the final handling of which was delayed for one reason or another. In fact Kashmir has not been solved as yet even today. During Nehru's lifetime, in spite of Patel's official portfolio in charge of the Indian States, it was Nehru who was the *de facto* Minister in charge of Kashmir, probably because everybody recognized him as of Kashmiri descent. Very soon it was Gopalaswamy Ayyangar, and then some others who were appointed as Ministers.

It is also a common knowledge that Kashmir was invaded by the tribals from Pakistan, and hastily acceded to India. Consequently, India sent her troops to save Srinagar, the capital city, from the invaders. It was, however, seldom asked why the accession to India was so delayed as to endanger the whole kingdom, which was on the brink of being occupied by the Pakistani forces, including both the tribal invaders and then its regular army.

Journalist Prem Shankar Jha, however, was bold enough to put a hypothesis as follows. Had Nehru been more accommodating, as Patel clearly wanted to be, Kashmir would have acceded to India well before the raiders invaded the state. The accession would have been incontestable not only on legal grounds, which were never in doubt, but what is more important, because it would demonstrably not have been under duress."[13]

Jha practically repeats the question in more detail toward the end of his book. "The most puzzling feature of the whole Kashmir affair has been Nehru's behaviour. The questions that generations of Indians have asked themselves about Nehru are: Why did he agree to making the accession conditional ? Why did he refer the dispute to the UNO ? Why did he accept the ceasefire when the Indian troops had gained the ascendancy, and when Muzaffarabad district, rural Poonch, and perhaps even Gilgit could have been retaken? To these we must now add new questions: Why did he reject the Maharaja's offer of accession in September when he himself had said to the Viceroy, Patel, and Gandhi, as late as 29 July, 1947, that Kashmir meant more to him than anything else? Why did he, for that matter, reject the Maharaja's offer again as late as 24 October? Why was he prepared to risk Srinagar rather than accept an offer that did not explicitly commit itself to the installation of a popular government under Sheikh Abdullah ?[14]

On a careful study of these problems, Jha arrived at the conclusion that "Thus Nehru's seemingly incomprehensible behaviour stemmed from the fact that he was trying to keep not just the ruler, but the people of Kashmir with India. Everything that Nehru did, especially his willingness to treat the accession as provisional, was geared to this purpose. Indeed, nowhere were Nehru's qualities of statesmanship more evident."[15]

Partition and the Communal Problem

Another crucial question at the time of independence was the communal issue. Shankar was strongly against the view that Patel was communal-minded. In his view, generally Gandhi and Nehru were thought to be pro-Muslim, and Patel seemed to be taking the side of Hindus and Sikhs. Even Judith Brown calls Patel "a Hindu nationalist".[16] In fact, "he told the Mahatma that Muslims not loyal to India should leave, and he could not help adding that he suspected a majority of disloyalty".[17] After the "Operation Polo" was over and the question of the Hyderabad State had been solved, however, he wrote to H.S. Suhrawardy (a Muslim League Premier of the undivided Bengal Province up to the partition) that "the Indian Union Muslims have come out in the open on our side and that has certainly created a good impression."[18]

On 30 September, 1947, a peak day of refugee migration both ways, Patel talked to the Sikh leaders at Amritsar so that a huge caravan of Muslim refugees on the way to Pakistan could safely cross the border, and this was the turning point in the whole tragedy concerning migration.[19] The other great sore in the communal issue was the refugees in the newly created West Bengal. This created a crisis in West Bengal in January 1950. For this, Liaqat Ali Khan, Pakistan's Prime Minister, was invited to come for negotiation and the Nehru-Liaqat Pact was concluded.

During the crisis, Nehru once conveyed to Patel of "the possibility of his going to East Bengal in a non-official capacity—in Gandhi like fashion—to see if he could stop the rot.[20] Around the same time, he also wrote to Vijayalakshmi Pandit, his sister and India's Ambassador to the US, that he wants to resign and go to Allahabad and Bengal, but "I really do not know what I shall do then" (SWJN-2, 14, Part I, 132-3). He could not hit upon any Gandhi-like idea. He was not supported by any mass organization, nor could he think of his own *Lok Sevak Sangh*. This was the difference between Gandhi and Nehru, and was the reason why Nehru did not have his own "*Hind Swaraj*" though he had produced his supreme *An Autobiography*. It was this aspect of Nehru that Bipan Chandra referred to in the above.

Then Patel visited Calcutta at Nehru's request and made an appeal to the people to give a fair trial to the Pact. He acted on this occasion as the supreme trouble shooter. B. Krishna called it his "last major historic act".[21]

As for the celebrated differences on communalism between the two, while Nehru took the stance of "absolute secularism", that of Patel was "diluted secularism".[22] At a Working Committee meeting back in April 1940, presumably soon after the Ramgarh Session of the Congress, "Heated discussion between Bapu (Patel) and Dr. Syed Mahmud who alleged that Congress has not paid any attention towards Mohammedans' grievances and have displeased them. Excited discussion-charges and counter-charges levelled against each other."[23]

Gandhi's Murder, Communalism, Constitution

Shortly before the assassination of Gandhi, Patel invited the RSS and the Hindu Mahasabha to join the Congress. Maniben wrote "A few RSS persons waited on Bapu" in her diary of 22 January, 1947, and these expressions were to be repeated thereafter. When Patel placed his Minority Committee's report on the table of the Constituent Assembly toward the end of May 1949, V.D. Savarkar, of Hindutva fame, sent a telegram "congratulating Bapu on the removal of reservation of seats for Minorities", meaning Muslims.[24] On the Muslim question Shankar says that 'then and even now' Patel is 'unfairly criticized',[25] and is called 'communalist'.[26] But 'merit and seniority' were his standard.[27]

According to Granville Austin, in the Constituent Assembly Patel was the Chairman of the Provincial Constitution Committee and of the Advisory Committee, while Nehru was the Chairman of the States Committee, of the Union Subjects Committee and of the Union Constitution Committee. The Minorities Sub-Committee was a sub-committee of the Advisory Committee and it was presumably as the Chairman of the latter that Patel produced the report as was described by Maniben.

Austin writes on the relation of Nehru and Patel at the Constitution-making stage that "Nehru and Patel were the focus of power in the Assembly...Each depended upon the other to complement his own abilities—Nehru on Patel perhaps more than Patel on Nehru...The two men spent an hour together in private conversation on most evenings and often settled matters on which they had differed during the day...The blend in the Constitution of idealistic provisions and articles of a practical, administrative, and technical nature is perhaps the best evidence of the joint influence of these two men." So, Nehru was the symbol of the idealistic provisions of the Constitution, and Patel of the articles of a practical, administrative, and technical nature. If they could spend time together in the evening, it must have been before Nehru's moving to his new residence, as was related before.[28]

When Gandhi was murdered, Nehru and Patel exchanged letters, the former's letter dated 3 February, 1948 and the latter's 5 February, and promised cooperation. In his letter Nehru expressed "in full loyalty to one another and with confidence in one another". Patel's reply began with "I am deeply touched, indeed overwhelmed, by the affection and warmth of your letter."

During the last year of Patel's life, there occurred a trouble at Ayodhya, Uttar Pradesh. Nehru's telegram to the Chief Minister of Uttar Pradesh, Govind Ballabh Pant, in December 1949 called Pant's attention to the installation on the night of 21 of that month of Ram and other Hindu images in Babri Masjid, the mosque which, it was said, had been built on the ruins of a Hindu temple and was thought to be the birthplace of Ram. It had therefore been locked by the Government (SWJN-2, 14, Part I, 443). There was an exchange of letters between Nehru and Rajaji. Patel, the Home Minister, was also coming to Lucknow at Pant's request, and it was made clear that all these four top Congressmen were keenly interested in the matter. Nehru wrote to Pant in April 1950 that "...the Uttar Pradesh is becoming almost a foreign land for me" (*Ibid.*, Part II, 293-4). The Ayodhya issue exploded in December 1992 in the form of the deliberate destruction of the Babari Masjid by a well-organized Hindu group, and has been simmering until this very day.

By the way, at Lucknow, the capital of Uttar Pradesh within several hours of driving from Ayodhya, the Pacific Conference, the Conference of the sister Institutes of Pacific Relations of about a dozen nations, was held in October 1950. Nehru spoke at its Inaugural session thus, "...we have suddenly arrived at the stage when we have to run-walking is not enough—and in running we stumble and fall..." (SWJN-2, 15, Part I, 500). The readers may be interested to know that a few decades ago a famous writer of Japan had used almost identical terms to describe the tasks facing Japan. The difference is that Nehru spoke for the whole of Asia. The Japanese writer did not. This is also the difference between one who has gone through the anti-colonial struggle for his nation and the people, and thereby acquired a wide view of the world, and one who has not.

If we look at the Nehru era, after the initial communal trouble which accompanied the partition, there followed almost a decade of relative communal peace. Then almost suddenly a fire broke out as a communal clash at the central Indian city of Jabalpur early in 1961, more than ten years after Patel's death. Nehru immediately wrote on 15 February to K.N. Katju, Chief Minister of Madhya Pradesh where Jabalpur is located, to call his attention to the relief for Muslim victims. He said, "I am deeply troubled with what has happened in Jabalpur, Sagar and other places in Madhya Pradesh. I am inclined to believe that there were organized and well laid-out plans for these attacks on Muslims and their houses" (SWJN-2, 67-107-8).

Two Presidential Elections

As Shankar saw it, as time went on "the previous warmth and openness (between the two) were absent."[29] But Patel himself saw it in a different way. He said that Nehru "had always been temperamental and a spoilt child; he had always got what he wanted; this was the second time he had failed (the first was his failure to get Rajaji elected as President) and he was naturally feeling the blow...".[30] Probably he was remembering what Motilal had asked him a long time ago (Motilal had died in 1931). On the election of the first President of India when India became a Republic, Patel thought that Rajendra Prasad was much more popular in the Congress, and thus opposed Nehru who strongly recommended Rajaji.

R.N.P. Singh writes that at the time of the Presidential election Nehru wrote to Prasad on 10 September, 1949 that he and Patel decided to support Rajaji, his opponent, which was baseless.[31]

According to Maniben's Diary, however, Patel's support to Prasad was surprisingly not necessarily unconditional. When his name was hinted, Patel was surprised, and said, "Rajendrababu no choice for that post. If he is installed he would influx whole house by Biharis."[32] Rajendra Prasad was from Bihar. In a similar vein Maniben writes about Maulana Azad, the Muslim Education Minister, that "whole of Education Department flooded with Mohammedans—Bapu told him that he was responsible for Bapuji's (Gandhi's) death", presumably by one-sidedly taking the side of the Muslim refugees.[33] Shankar writes, by the way, that Prasad, and for that matter Pant were particularly deferential to Sardar, "the former had the attitude of a younger brother and the latter of a disciple."[34] Shankar says nothing on Patel's attitude toward the Somnath Temple in Gujarat on the reconstruction of which Prasad was said to be very keen. It was in March 1951, after Patel's death, that Prasad requested Nehru to inaugurate the Temple which had been reconstructed entirely by private subscriptions (SWJN-2,16, Part I, 603).

When it came to the choice of the Congress President for 1950, it became a fight between Purushottam Das Tandon and Acharya Kripalani, and the former, supported by Patel and Pant, defeated the latter, but not with a considerable margin, who had got the support of Nehru. This was 'the second time'. Patel said that until the election of Tandon, and until Nehru gave his ear to Rafi Ahmed Kidwai, Maulana Azad and Mridula Sarabhai, his close friends, he had been on good terms with Nehru. When Tandon was elected, Nehru at first refused to sit in his Working Committee. A compromise was made, however, and Tandon announced the 20 names of his Committee on 16 October (SWJN-2, 15, Part I, 152, fn2). This was while Patel was alive. But Nehru was not co-operative, to say the least. In his letter to Tandon in May 1951, for example, he wrote, "Important issues are not discussed in the Congress itself or in the AICC, but are considered by odd individuals or small groups privately. This seems to me a wrong approach which might progressively vitiate our politics" (SWJN-2, 16, Part I, 343). We have seen Nehru's similar reproach before. There was no more Patel at this time. Nehru, moreover, submitted his resignation from the Working Committee in August 1951 (SWJN-2, 16, Part II, 155), and by doing so forced Tandon to resign. He got elected the Congress President himself.

These two elections have sufficiently shown Sardar's influence within the Congress. There is one more thing which impressed Shankar of Patel's influence on a very different occasion. In order to have a rest, the weakening Patel, together with Maniben and Shankar, were sent cruising on an Indian warship from Bombay along the western coast down to Trivandrum. This was in May 1950. Then, "The meetings provided me with yet another insight into Sardar's hold on Congressmen in far-off places. I found that all the leading lights of these places (Shankar mentions Karwar and Mangalore, both in the present Karnataka) were well-known to Sardar who not only recognized them but exchanged anecdotes of olden days."[35]

Nehru's Style Again

Did Nehru generally listen to others' views? When Nehru, for example, spoke on the radio that the opinion of the people of Jammu & Kashmir would be ascertained "under U.N. auspices", Patel, who had some mental reservations on this issue, had not been consulted well in advance.[36] By the way Shankar writes that it was on 28 October, 1947. *The Essential Writings of Jawaharlal Nehru,* edited by historian S. Gopal, says that Nehru's "Broadcast on Kashmir", containing the phrase "a referendum held under international auspices like the United Nations", was made on 2 November.[37] The broadcast was in consonance with, for example, what the British Prime Minister wanted. In his letter to Nehru at the end of the year, Clement Attlee wrote that the settlement in Kashmir must be made "only under the authority of the United Nations"(SWJN-2, 4-419, fn2). One wonders if there was any collaboration between Mountbatten, the Governor-General, and the British Government, taking India hostage and depriving India of her freedom of action.

Shankar also writes on the resignation of Finance Minister John Mathai over the setting up of the Planning Commission that "Sardar was unhappy about it but he knew that Pandit Nehru did not take kindly to any one crossing his path and particularly if it was done with strength and boldness as Mathai was used to doing."[38] B. Krishna quotes Mathai who said that the Cabinet System did not function under Nehru. It did, as far as he was concerned, only when Patel was the Acting Prime Minister in October 1948 (the first of the four times he was the Acting Prime Minister).[39] This was, generally speaking, Nehru's style. Also Gopalaswamy Ayyangar was made a Minister in *de facto* charge of Jammu & Kashmir and Pakistan, without Nehru consulting Patel, who was the Minister of States. Patel said, "when he (Nehru) goes out, he leaves written instructions, that Kashmir, External Affairs be looked after by Gopalaswamy. How can then interfere?"[40] Maniben also recorded her father thus, "Foreign Affairs Committee, he (Nehru) never consults us. After dispatching telegrams and instructions, he sends copies for our information only."[41]

Publishers' Note to Vol. 1 of *Sardar Patel's Correspondence* says that "From August 1946 he (Patel) was nominated by the Congress Working Committee in association with Maulana Azad to pursue this matter (Kashmir) from the point where Nehru had left it on account of his preoccupation with the Cabinet Mission." It also says, "For Sardar, Kashmir was a subject for the States Ministry, Nehru thought that international issues were involved in it. That caused the difference between the approaches of the two. The Sardar, therefore, had practically little hand in the affairs of Kashmir after December '47'.[42]

This style was at its worst when Nehru, with the help of almost Krishna Menon alone, made decisions on diplomatic and military affairs in 1962, as will be discussed later in this book. India's *Outlook* magazine, in the article on The Dramatis Personae in its fiftieth-year Anniversary 22 October, 2012 Number of the 1962 war, wrote that against China's five the Indian politicians in charge were only two, Nehru and Krishna Menon.

Srinath Raghavan, a former Indian Army officer, writes in the same Number that on the Sino-Indian border problem Krishna Menon alone was of the view that negotiations with China were really needed for its solution. He was having a crucial talk with China's Foreign Minister Chen I at Geneva shortly before the war, and they seemed to have reached an agreement. But Nehru's approval did not come in time.[43] This story would be told again later on the basis of Menon's biography. Would it be a waste of time to ask what would have happened if Menon had had his own independent mandate as, for example, the Minister for External Affairs?

Another instance of this style was that it had been understood that both Ayyangar and Rajaji on one occasion or another would be made Foreign Minister, but actually both became Ministers without portfolio. This would suggest that Nehru would not have even a man of Rajaji's status as his Foreign Policy Adviser, to make the whole of that area his own ground. In his new cabinet when India became independent, his portfolios were External Affairs and Commonwealth Relations and Scientific Research. He was his own Foreign Minister till the end. One can imagine how that has added to his burden of work, especially at a war-time. It is interesting to know, by the way, that in his letter to C.D. Deshmukh in 1951, Nehru listed Krishna Menon, Vijayalakshmi Pandit, Panikkar and Radhakrishnan as India's four 'first-rate' diplomats (SWJN-2, 16, Part II, 745). This list is surprising, as Patel would have taken none of them. He said of Vijayalakshmi that she, India's Ambassador to the US at the time, "continues to quarrel with all".[44]

Nehru read a Statement on Vallabhbhai Patel in the Parliament, when Patel died, saying that "he...would not have liked us to leave our work and just go in large number to Bombay..." (SWJN-2, 15, Part II, 654-5). Would it be less than fair to Nehru to conclude from this that he did not want to be put on equal footing with Patel at the end of the day? The Resolution mourning the death of Patel drafted by Nehru for the Cabinet says, among others, "In particular, his genius was demonstrated in the way he handled the difficult and complicated problem of the old Indian States."[45] Somehow it gives the feeling of lacking in enthusiasm. But, the next AICC was held at Ahmedabad at the end of January 1951, as Patel had invited it on behalf of that city.

The famous letter by Patel to Nehru on Tibet will be taken up in Chapter 9.

Notes

1. Shankar, V., *My Reminiscences of Sardar Patel*, I, 8.
2. Brown, Judith, *Nehru*, 25.
3. Shankar, V., *My Reminiscences of Sardar Patel*, II, 163.
4. *Ibid.*
5. *Sardar Patel's Correspondence*, Vol. 2, xlvii.
6. Patel, Maniben, *Inside Story of Sardar Patel*, 32.
7. Gandhi, Rajmohan, *Patel*, 491.
8. Shankar, V., *My Reminiscences of Sardar Patel*, I, 156.
9. *Ibid.*, I, 179.
10. Nehru, *The Essential Writings of Jawaharlal Nehru*, II, 645.
11. Shankar, V., *My Reminiscences of Sardar Patel*, I, 66.
12. *Sardar Patel's Correspondence*, Vol. 8, 404.
13. Jha, Prem Shankar, *Kashmir 1947*, 46.
14. *Ibid.*, 124.
15. *Ibid.*, 126.
16. Brown, Judith, *Nehru*, 73.
17. Gandhi, Rajmohan, *Patel*, 431.
18. *Ibid.*, 483.
19. Shankar, V., *My Reminiscences of Sardar Patel*, I, 104-5, 106, 140-1.
20. *Ibid.*, II, 85.
21. Krishna, B., *Sardar Vallabhbhai Patel*, 501-11.
22. Shankar, V., *My Reminiscences of Sardar Patel*, I, 91.

23. Patel, Maniben, *Inside Story of Sardar Patel*, 115.
24. *Ibid.*, 278.
25. Shankar, V., *My Reminiscences of Sardar Patel*, I, 192.
26. *Ibid.*, II, 173.
27. *Ibid.*, 174.
28. Austin, Granville, *The Indian Constitution*, 315.
29. Shankar, V., *My Reminiscences of Sardar Patel*, II, 143.
30. *Ibid.*
31. Singh, R.N.P., *Nehru*, 167-8.
32. Patel, Maniben, *Inside Story of Sardar Patel*, 295-7.
33. *Ibid.*, 365.
34. Shankar, V., *My Reminiscences of Sardar Patel*, II, 24.
35. *Ibid.*, II, 98.
36. *Ibid.*, I, 133-4.
37. Nehru, *The Essential Writings of Jawaharlal Nehru*, II, 329.
38. Shankar, V., *My Reminiscences of Sardar Patel*, II, 97.
39. Krishna, B., *Sardar Vallabhbhai Patel*, 505.
40. Patel, Maniben, *Inside Story of Sardar Patel*, 274.
41. *Ibid.*, 386.
42. *Sardar Patel's Correspondence*, Vol.1, ix-x.
43. "The Dramatis Personae", Srinath Raghavan, *Outlook*, Anniversary Number, 22 October 2012.
44. Patel, Maniben, *Inside Story of Sardar Patel*, 458.
45. Nehru, *The Essential Writings of Jawaharlal Nehru*, I, 623.

8
"Free of Attachment to Blocs"—Nehru's Foreign Policy

"India is the Pivot"

It is difficult to say, rather to our surprise, that, though Nehru, or for that matter India, have been strongly identified with the policy of non-alignment, Nehru's mind was wholly preoccupied with this idea from the beginning of independence. On 5 September, 1946, only three days after he had been appointed as the Vice-President of the Viceroy's Executive Council, the *de facto* Prime Minister, he prepared a Note titled "The United Nations". It was so titled because it was written in order to prepare the Indian Government to apply for a non-permanent membership in the UN Security Council.

There Nehru wrote, "Whatever the present position of India might be, she is potentially a Great Power. Undoubtedly, in future she will have to play a very great part in security problems of Asia and the Indian Ocean, more especially of the Middle East and South-East Asia. Indeed, India is the pivot round which these problems will have to be considered" (*SWJN-2*, 1-439, also quoted in Srinath Raghavan's *India's War*). The Middle East and South East Asia are specially mentioned here because these were the battlegrounds for the Indian Army during the Second World War which had just been concluded. Nehru was apparently speaking on the basis of India's own experience in the war. He was not directly talking of the military dimension, or of India as a military power. But, it is difficult not to notice the security (military) element in the Note. One wonders if the thought of power politics is not hiding here, though the situation did not develop along these lines.

In his "Note on Defence" written about a week later, which was referred to already, Nehru mentions Japan, Hong Kong, Malaya, Thailand, the Dutch East Indies, Burma, Borneo, Ceylon, Iraq, Middle East, and Italy as the places from where the Indian Army was now to be withdrawn, with special emphasis on the Dutch East Indies and Iraq (SWJN-2, 3- 491-2). This special emphasis corresponds to the mention of the Middle East and South-East Asia in the first Note.

About six months afterwards, there was an Asian Relations Conference in Delhi, practically convened by Nehru, where 243 delegates from 28 countries were invited. Part of Nehru's speech at its plenary session ran as follows. "...she (India) is the natural centre and focal point of the many forces at work in Asia...geographically she is so situated as to be the meeting point of Western and Northern and Eastern and South-East Asia" (SWJN-2, 2-506). The security question may not be as apparent here, but the idea that India is a great power is still very much dormant.

Shift to the Non-Alignment Policy

From here Nehru's thinking seems to have gradually moved to that of what we now-a-days usually associate with the concept of non-alignment. It has to a large extent depended to the rise of other Asian countries, like Indonesia and China. As the first Republic Day in 1950 was approaching, Nehru wrote to Chief Ministers that "We have also decided not to invite prominent statesmen or others from abroad on this occasion. There is one exception, however, and that is of President Soekarno of the Indonesian Republic" (LCM, 1-489). India had been encouraging the independence struggle of the Indonesian people against the Dutch. At the same time the evolution of the Cold War, especially embodied in Asia by the Korean War, was forcing Nehru, and the like-minded people, to the position of non-alignment. One is also reminded here of what John Garver said of India, which was quoted at the end of Chapter 2.

We will see from his letters and so on how this idea of non-alignment has gradually taken shape. He writes, for instance, that "gradually new alignments take place outside those dominant spheres. This does not mean, as has sometimes been suggested, that a "third force" or a new power bloc is taking shape" (LCM, 3—72-73). Or,

"Keeping apart, we, and such other countries as function in the same way, at least keep an area free from the fever of war and can view events with some calmness and objectivity, and occasionally throw out weight on the side of peace. Thus,...the only policy we can pursue is one of non-alignment with the power blocs and trying to maintain friendly relations with all countries" (*Ibid.*, 87). Also, "If again war breaks out, in spite of endeavours to the contrary, then we shall keep out of it and try to keep as many other countries as possible out of it also" (*Ibid.*, 236).

Those three letters were written from 1952 to 1953, during the Korean War. The readers may be interested to know that the title of this Chapter, "free of attachment to blocs", has been taken from one of the earliest such expressions, in 1948, by Nehru (LCM, 1-69). Nehru was not under the illusion that India alone could do a lot in this direction. He wrote that "I realize that, in the circumstances prevailing today, India's capacity to influence them is strictly limited." But he continued, "Nevertheless, there is a possibility of making a difference and that difference may be between war and peace" (LCM, 2-144). To make a difference between war and peace is a great and worthy ambition.

On 30 September, 1950, as the US Army in their counter-offensive came up near the 38th parallel from the south, Nehru warned against their crossing it (*Ibid.*, 218). The Chinese Premier Zhou En-lai told the Indian Ambassador the next day that if they crossed the line, China would have to support North Korea (*Ibid.*). China here was apparently using India as their interpreter with the world. Against this background, Nehru said that "Briefly put, the two major international problems today are Korea and Germany" (LCM, 3-101). At the time of writing, Korea still remains divided. Germany remained so till 1990. As Nehru saw it, "In the Korean deadlock, attempts are made on both sides to utilize India's services to help to resolve it" (LCM, 3—311, the ceasefire was made effective on 27 July, 1953). From the above it is clear that his non-alignment has emerged under the impact of the Korean War to a great extent. Also, the possibility of China's involvement, together with her Soviet connection, must have called his attention.

On the Middle East, Nehru's observation after a brief visit there on his way home from Europe in June 1953 was that "There is no doubt that in Egypt, as well as in the entire Middle East, India is looked up to, to some extent, as a guide and a friend" (*Ibid.*, 330). Journalist M.J. Akbar writes in his biography of Nehru that 1955 was "his finest year"[2], and he was 'at his best' at the time of the Suez War.[3] S. Gopal also says in his *Jawaharlal Nehru: A Biography* that the Suez showed Nehru's best.[4] Indeed, "When people talk about neutral nations, the first country they think of is India" (LCM, 3-553).

In mid-1955 the Soviet Union proposed an epoch-making plan for Germany. Nehru would have supported it under the usual circumstances. But in this case he had to say that "The Soviet conception of a neutral united Germany was not acceptable to the West and, for all practical purposes, cannot be considered feasible now" (LCM, 4-173, 238).

The Soviet plan reminds us of an article Professor Nambara Shigeru, a Japanese political philosopher, wrote in a monthly journal (in Japanese) to commemorate Japan's admission into the UN at the end of 1956. Nambara observed that the reconciliation with China and friendship with the newly emerging countries of "Asia, Arabia and the African Continent" were the foremost tasks before Japan, and it would be difficult for her to find her way through without the trust and confidence of those nations. He was critical of Japan's military alliance with the US. About Europe he suggested that Germany should be united and neutralized, thus creating a spacious zone of peace right in the central Europe. This was clearly an example of Japan-based thought of non-alignment.

Peace Treaty with Japan

Nehru's policy towards the Peace Treaty with Japan shows how his non-alignment came to be formed in one important aspect. In his *Letters to Chief Ministers* he made his first reference to this problem on 22 July, 1951 (LCM, 2-453-4). There he wrote that "A really satisfactory treaty should have included China and Soviet Russia". The Korean War was still being fought and China had participated on a large scale, leaving the US the only major actor for drafting the Peace Treaty with Japan. In his next reference to the question Nehru expressed his criticism of the Anglo-American draft of the Treaty, and said that "The result is likely to be that we shall not join this multilateral treaty, as we cannot concur in some of its provisions...In such an event, we would prefer to have a simple bilateral treaty with Japan" (LCM, 2-465). India was against, among others, the probable exclusion of the above-mentioned two countries, which would leave Asia permanently divided, and "the failure to restore Taiwan to China, and the presence of foreign troops in Japan after the occupation had ended" (*Ibid.*, fn12). It is remarkable that Nehru's attention was keenly attracted to Taiwan. He said, for example, after the US declared to back up Taiwan militarily and the PRC had sent troops to Korea, "Formosa (Taiwan) indeed has become the crux of the question in the Far East" (*Ibid.*, 301). In the end, as "our major proposals were rejected...Hence, we are not sending any representative to the San Francisco Conference" (*Ibid.*, 483). More generally Nehru commented, shall we say as a historian, "The old practice of deciding about Asian questions in Europe and America, and not thinking too much of the opinion of Asian countries, still holds" (*Ibid.*, 484).

Thus, the Peace Treaty with Japan was signed in September 1951, without India attending. So, was the US-Japan Security Treaty on the same day. An article in the former was so framed that Japan was allowed to conclude a military alliance with a foreign country, and the US occupation forces would continue to remain in the country under a different name. Japan also signed a bilateral treaty with Taiwan in April 1952, and with India in June the same year. These together, as Nehru had anticipated, conditioned Japan's international stance for a very long time to come, in many ways even to this day. It was only in 1978 that Japan signed the Peace Treaty with the PRC. Japan also has had a great deal of difficulty with normalizing relations with both Koreas. There is still no formal relation with the DPRK (North Korea) as of today.

Nehru's Japan Visit

Nehru visited Japan from 4 to 13 October, 1957, and dictated his impressions on his way home (LCM, 4-564-580). He wrote about many things, for example, the school-going population being nearly a quarter of the total, the difference in school enrolment ratio between male and female in high schools and especially in the universities after the nine years of compulsory education, for every five male university students there was only one female (now the ratio is about the same), school uniforms, the same education all over the country, school meals, school excursion for visiting famous places, "an exaggerated courtesy which is very pleasing", punctuality, no display of gold or silver. There is nothing here on the Yen credit to be provided by Japan.

He also wrote that "...nowhere have I received such a big and spontaneous welcome as in Japan" (SWJN-2, 39-614). Also, "But I do think that it represented a broad reaction to India's foreign policy of peace and friendship. What was the significance, I often wondered, of this very warm welcome that the Japanese people gave me...the fear of the nuclear explosions...In this matter I think that the Japanese Government lags very much behind public opinion in Japan" (*Ibid.*, 622-3).

Nehru was correct. It may be added that in Japan at that time the forces hostile to some Articles of the Constitution, especially Article 9 prohibiting any war potential, were raising their head. If they had got a two-third majority in the 1955 Elections to the Lower House of Parliament, they might well have thought that the time for Constitutional Amendment had come. This is not to say that Nehru's policy directly influenced Japanese politics. But such must have been in the mind of those Japanese who gave him a big welcome. On the Constitution of Japan itself Nehru once said, according to the Minutes of the sixth meeting of the Commonwealth Prime Ministers, that "Mr. Nehru said that in his view Japan would be well advised not to alter the existing provision in her Constitution which forbade her to rearm." This was on 9 January, 1951, several months before the Peace Treaty problem came up, (SWJN-2, 15, Part 2,584).

We will briefly look at the subsequent relations between India and Japan after Nehru's 1957 visit. In a way, it was the peak year of the relations. For one thing there was the Indo-Chinese conflict. It was disappointing to see Nehru losing a war. It was even more so to see him fight a war at all, and practically on two fronts, China and Pakistan. Probably more important in diminishing the image of India in the Japanese mind at that time was the quick rise of the NICS (Newly Industrializing Countries) like South Korea, Taiwan, Hong Kong and Singapore from the mid-1960s, roughly at the same time as Nehru's demise. Their rise was more or less politically motivated. South Korea with the largest population among the four was a good example.

The military-dictatorial elite groups of that country, the so-called KT Group, re-established relations with Japan by the Treaty of 1965, got the Japanese Government to back them up for a forced industrialization centred round some large-scale engineering projects like the steel mills at Pohan on the East coast, and achieved "the Han River's miracle". In the process every sign of democratic movement was suppressed, symbolized by the Gwanju Incident of May 1980 which suppressed the emerging "Seoul Spring".

Some Government scholars and intellectuals tried to theorize that it was not possible to have democracy until the economic growth reached a certain level, a point we have already discussed. This so-called "modernization theory" was made use of by the dictatorial elites almost all over the world. Nehru would have nothing to do with it, but after Nehru even in India it had some audience. What took place in the four NICS gradually spread to some ASEAN countries, and it was natural that India's image in this picture gradually diminished. One important index of this shrinkage was that the amount of trade between India and Japan stagnated at about $4 billion for a long time.

What about the Sino-Japanese relations, then? There is also politics here. China was not, as we have seen, invited to the Peace Conference. The US thus successfully kept the distance between Japan and Communist China. They also inspired Japan and South Korea to approach each other and negotiate. As the Vietnam War continued and intensified, however, the US drastically changed their China policy and made friends with them, and that also led to the rehabilitation of the relations between Japan and China.

Shashi Tharoor on Nehru

To end this chapter, we will have a look at some portions of the last chapter of Shashi Tharoor's well thought-out work, *Nehru: The Invention of India*.

According to him, "Nehru's impact on India rested on four major pillars—democratic institution-building, staunch pan-Indian secularism, socialist economics at home and foreign policy of non-alignment."[5] But "Of the four major pillars of his system, two—democratic institution-building and staunch secularism—were indispensable to the country's survival as a pluralist land; a third, non-alignment, preserved its self-respect and enhanced its international standing without bringing any concrete benefits to the Indian people; the fourth, socialist economics, was disastrous, condemning the Indian people to poverty and stagnation and engendering inefficiency, red tapism and corruption on a scale rarely rivalled elsewhere...democracy endures, secularism is besieged, non-alignment is all but forgotten, and socialism barely clings on."[6] This was his evaluation of Nehru as of 2003.

The author is not particularly against Tharoor's argument. Concerning the non-alignment out of the four pillars, however, the author believes that it has still got an important role to play in the presence of powerful military alliances in the world. Moreover, as several people who have been quoted have pointed out, the Non-Aligned Movement (NAM) has played a considerable role in preventing the Cold War from turning hot, and Nehru's place in it is by no means to be easily 'forgotton'. In this sense it may be said to have brought a great deal of benefit to the people everywhere, if not in the form of tangible day-to-day necessities. Needless to say, and as has been pointed out in the above, the latter should also have been provided.

Notes

1. Raghavan, Srinath, *India's War*, 455.
2. Akbar, M.J., *Nehru*, 495.
3. *Ibid.*, 501.
4. Gopal, S., *Jawaharlal Nehru*, Vol. 2, 290.
5. Tharoor, Shashi, *Nehru*, 220.
6. *Ibid.*, 251.

9
Could the 1962 War Have Been Averted?

Conditions for Avoiding the War

In his previous book the author has pointed out three factors which could have averted the Indo-Chinese War of 1962. In a little modified form they were,

1. If China had conveyed her views on the Indo-Chinese border to India that there was indeed a border dispute, a potentially serious one, at least two or three years ago, the two governments could have discussed the issue in a much calmer atmosphere. The so-called Chinese old maps were a part of the problem and should have been discussed as well. On this point China clearly deceived India by saying that they did not have time to make new ones when they apparently had no such intention. There could have been a peaceful exchange of territories, though Nehru was saying he was against such a barter.

2. The Opposition parties in India should have restrained their attack on Nehru, so that Nehru would not have been cornered into a position where he could not make any compromise on the border question even if he had wanted to, and had no other alternative but to fight China militarily and defeat it.

3. The political asylum to the Dalai Lama should not have been given so easily. The Dalai Lama had been to India before at Nehru's invitation in late 1956, about two and a half years before the asylum, and it was very natural that he was seen as a friend of India, especially of Nehru. But at the very least Nehru should not have got in touch with him so soon after the asylum was granted and in such cordial atmosphere (in Delhi three weeks after the asylum). Also the Dalai

Lama should not have been given such freedom of activities as he was. On his part, the Dalai Lama, if he calls himself a Gandhian, should not have asked for asylum remembering that Gandhi always advised the refugees to return to the place of their origin.[1] He also should not have received the Nobel Peace Prize (in 1989) while he was in India. Or he should not have published a Constitution of Tibet in India. China protested against it in a Note of 25 March, 1963. According to S. Gopal's biography, among Nehru's top advisers only Krishna Menon had reservations about giving asylum to him.[2] Menon saw Pakistan as a greater threat than China, and valued China's friendship more highly than others.

Guha's Interpretations

These points may not have been enough to avoid the war as they are besides the main border issue. We will look into it in more detail. But before going into the details of the border question, we will see what historian Ramachandra Guha writes in his bulky book *India After Gandhi*. At least at two places in the book Guha tries to interpret in his own way what China said to India, and what Zhou En-lai said to Nehru on the issue.

One is on Zhou's letters to Nehru of 7 November and 17 December, 1959. In Guha's view, "stripped of its diplomatic code", they read, "You keep your (possibly fraudulently acquired—Guha) territory in the East, while we shall keep our (possibly fraudulently acquired—Guha) territory in the West."[3] (also *see* SWJN-2, 54-663-6, 55-321-3).

Second is on Zhou's final visit to Delhi in April 1960, when he told Nehru that "in the eastern sector, we acknowledge that what India considers its border has been reached by India's actual administration. But, similarly, we think that India should accept that China's administrative personnel has reached the line which it considers to be her border in the western sector."[4] The Eastern sector means the McMahon Line, and the Western sector Aksai Chin.

What Guha writes here is the crux of the matter of the border question between the two countries. Guha may or may not be suggesting the exchange of these territories between the two. It would not be easy at this moment anyway. But if Nehru and his advisers, instead of sticking to the fixed position that the disputed territories both in the East and the West belonged to India and are not negotiable, which has inevitably led to a similarly rigid stance of China, had been big-minded enough to look at the situation in more or less the same way as the Chinese side, the war could well have been averted, and the matter of national humiliation would certainly not have arisen. What S. Gopal writes in Nehru's biography is also interesting. He says that if India had agreed that there was a room for negotiation, it alone could well have saved China's face.

We will also consider one thing more that Guha said in this connection, which is that "In retrospect, it appears that the Indians underestimated the force of Chinese resentment against "Western imperialism", in this case the British imperialism in particular. In the first half of the twentieth century, when their country was weak, it had been subject to all sorts of indignities by the European powers. The McMahon Line was one of them."[5]

Here is also what Mao Zedong told a Nepali delegation in 1964, after theIndo-Chinese fighting was over. He said that in India-China relations "The major problem is not the problem of the McMahon line, but the Tibet question", although as Garver says these two are closely mixed up in the Eastern sector of the boundary.[6]

India and Tibet

The border question immediately after India's independence of 1947 and the Chinese revolution of 1949 was broadly as follows.[7] India advanced to Tawang in NEFA in 1951, which was to the south of the McMahon Line. Therefore, it was as if China admitted India's advance to the said Line. A little earlier, Nehru said in the Lok Sabha concerning the border of India and Tibet that in the East it was the McMahon Line, and in the West it had been determined "by long usage and custom". Zhou En-lai told the Indian Ambassador to China in September 1951 that there was "no territorial dispute" between the two countries. This could also be taken as a sign of China's acceptance of the McMahon Line as the border.

At the Asian Relations Conference shortly before India's independence, the Chinese Delegation was, as Benjamin Zachariah points out in his Nehru, still represented by the Guomindang. They "had insisted that questions of Tibet's political status should not be discussed" at the Conference.[8] Was it Nehru's intention at all to discuss it and reach some conclusion in India's favour? The author is not aware of any such evidence. But the British had occupied the Tawang Tract by 1947.[9] China wanted to negotiate with India, but India said the frontier was not negotiable and there could be no compromise. In 1954 the Indian maps depicted Aksai Chin as part of India. S. Gopal said after research in London that India was in an advantageous position compared to China as far as the territory of Aksai Chin was concerned.

Incidentally Nehru, at the request of Mountbatten, prepared "A Note on Kashmir" in June 1947, shortly before independence. In that Note he says that Kashmir consists of three parts: Kashmir proper, Jammu, and Ladakh, Baltistan, Skardu and Kargil. It is a matter of regret that he did not bother to delineate those areas he included in the third part, particularly if in his notion Ladakh includes Aksai Chin or not. Would it be possible that it was not in his picture of Kashmir at all? (SWJN-2, 3- 222-9).

On the possible threat from China to India, exactly two months after the PRC had been established, Nehru wrote to the Chief Ministers on 1 December, 1949 that "India is not directly affected in the sense of any military danger. It is possible that the Chinese Communist regime may spread to Tibet...Even if it so spreads, there is no military danger from that quarter to India...One thing is dead clear. We will not permit the slightest intervention, aggression or invasion of any Indian territory wherever it might be" (LCM, 1—485-6). Very soon afterwards, on 30 December, India recognized the PRC. When the Korean War broke out in June the next year, Nehru said the PRC should be brought into the UN in order to prevent the spread of the conflict (LCM, 2—124). Certainly at the time of the 1962 war it would have been much better for India to have China sitting in the UN, as it would have been much more approachable.

On India's interest in Tibet, Nehru said, "Our position has been that we recognize the suzerainty of China over Tibet, but at the same time we believe that Tibet should retain her full autonomy. Further that the special trade and other interests that India has in Tibet should continue" (*Ibid.*, 187). To hope that Tibet should retain her autonomy, one may wonder, might amount to intervention in China's internal affairs. Similarly, it would have been much better not to hope for the protection of India's special interest. But in October 1950, just one year after the establishment of the new state, Chinese troops entered Tibet. Nehru wrote, "I must say that this action of the Chinese Government has hurt us considerably..." (*Ibid.*, 236-7). As he saw it, "From a military point of view, this has not great consequence and involves no particular danger to India", but "we shall always keep proper watch on our extended frontiers..."(*Ibid.*, 239). He said, "Ever since this development in Tibet, there has been much talk in India about threats to our frontier. I think that there is no foreseeable possibility of any real military threat to our frontier *via* Tibet" (*Ibid.*, 281).

Patel's and Douratram's Letters

By this time the above-mentioned Sardar Patel's letter on Tibet must have been delivered, and Nehru must have got it in mind. But he reiterated his stand sometime later in this way, "I do not think there is the slightest danger of a military invasion from or *via* Tibet" (*Ibid.*, 292).

We will analyse Patel's letter a little.[10] It was addressed to Nehru and dated 7 November, 1950, only about five weeks before his death. He started by saying that he had given much thought to the Tibet question and "I thought I should share with you what is passing through my mind" as China came near "almost up to our gates".

As Sardar Patel saw it, "The Chinese Government have tried to delude us by professions of peaceful intentions...The tragedy of it is that the Tibetans put faith in us...Our Ambassador has been at great pains to find an explanation or justification for Chinese policy and actions."

At the same time China thinks that "our attitude is determined by foreign influences." The difficulties are that "The undefined state of the frontier and the existence on our side of a population with its affinities to Tibetans or Chinese have all the elements of potential trouble between China and ourselves." India also has to consider the possibility of China and Pakistan coming closer, to build 'two fronts' or 'double threat'.

Finally, Patel lists about a dozen items for India to think about, and says that "I suggest that we meet early to have a general discussion on these problems...".

We may notice that he was of the view that India's frontier was undefined, which was interestingly the same as the official Chinese view. So is his view that Tibetans or Chinese, and by implication not the tribals, are among the residents on the Indian side. Patel's list also includes "The question of Chinese entry into UNO". This means "I am doubtful whether we can advocate its claims any longer." He is putting it not only in connection with India, but also in connection with China's participation in the Korean War. The last item in the list is "The policy in regard to the McMahon Line", but he has not given his view on the Line here.

As if to reply to Patel's letter, Nehru wrote "Prime Minister Nehru's Note on China and Tibet" on 18 November.[11] The main points of this Note are, in Tibet a large measure of autonomy is almost inevitable, he rules out any major attack on India by China, if we fall out completely with China, Pakistan will undoubtedly try to take advantage of this, politically or otherwise, and the real protection we should seek is some kind of understanding of China. The last point is crucially important, because, unlike Patel, Nehru was of the opinion that the border of the two countries are solidly defined and not for negotiation, and therefore, talks on the border issue are not a part of the 'understanding' in his mind. This Note is not in the SWJN-2. The meeting suggested by Patel did not come true. It may not be possible to look at this Note as a reply to Patel's letter as the latter has been written in more concrete terms.

V. Shankar wrote that Patel "felt so keenly about the problem that he asked me to draft a letter to Pandit Nehru...". When Shankar showed him a draft, Patel approved of it with some amendments and got it sent. Patel showed it to Gopalaswami Ayyangar and Girija Shankar Bajpai from the External Affairs Ministry.[12] The author has meta person who told him that it was Bajpai who drafted the letter. Anyway Nehru did not answer it.

It would be useful to see the three letters Assam Governor Jairamdas Doulatram wrote to Patel, the Home Minister, on the same day, 26 November, 1950, although only two of them are to be found in Vol. 9 of *Sardar Patel's Correspondence*. These letters are very keen on the problems of defence of the North East Frontiers of India.

Jairamdas writes, "I believe that the whole problem of defence of our border against Chinese incursion is being considered at Delhi at the highest level and that the highest Army officials would be busy completing the necessary defence arrangements...The terrain is so unfamiliar except to the Assam Rifles officers...The North East frontier hills are regarded on all hands as the most difficult terrain for fighting...Our regular Army officers and men have never been to these North-East hills and both will be dealing with not only a difficult terrain, occupied by people little known to them...".[13] These letters were of as much worth as Patel's own calling attention regarding the defence of India. But Patel who got them was already a fatally ill man by this time, Maniben having written in her diary 'Pain in stomach' on 15 November from which he never recovered. Patel wrote a brief acknowledgement to Jairamdas, conveying him that he had drawn the attention of the Defence Secretary, H.M. Patel, to the subject.[14]

Old Chinese Maps

Concerning the frontier issue, Nehru was certain from the beginning that "About our frontier, the McMahon Line, we are adamant and we are not going to tolerate any breach of it" (LCM, 2-268). He also said, "our frontier with Tibet, known as the McMahon Line, was our fixed and definite border and we were not prepared to consider any change in it" (LCM, 3-74).

To a question in Parliament on some Chinese maps, • Nehru replied that "our maps show that the McMahon Line is our boundary and that is our boundary-map or no map" (LCM, 2-302fn4). The question says that Chinese maps showed China's boundaries extending down to the Brahmaputra river (*Ibid.*). Nehru said that "It has been pointed out to us by the Chinese authorities that these maps are old maps and they do not rely upon them. They have had no time to draw new maps" (LCM, 2-302). If we look back today, what the Chinese authorities told the Indian side was not true, they drew what they believed to be the Chinese territory as such on their maps, and had no intention to redraw them. Therefore, they, including Zhou En-lai, deceived the Indian Government. They did the same thing when they said that there was no territorial dispute between the two countries.

But, why is it that the Indian Government did not want to formally ratify, together with China, the boundary at this time, the McMahon Line or whatever? Since China did not protest against India's claim in these earlier years of contact, India could well have taken the opportunity to ask China formally to agree to the Indian conception of the border. This is what people like Ramachandra Guha is talking about as is shown before, though his examples were related to somewhat later years, 1959 and 1960. The two countries held negotiations on Tibet from the end of 1953 till well into 1954. The Indo-Chinese Agreement on Tibet, signed on 29 April, 1954, contained *Panchsheel* principles. Nehru and Zhou confirmed these principles in a Joint Statement issued at the end of their talks in Delhi in June 1954, which made these principles world-famous. Surprisingly, Nehru wrote, just prior to the Tibet Conference, that "What is of essential consequence is our frontier and by that we will stand. Indeed, we do not propose to discuss this matter" (LCM, 3-459). Or, he wrote after the Conference that "on this matter we were not prepared to parley with anyone, and I declared publicly in Parliament and elsewhere that this frontier, including the McMahon Line was a firm one and was not open to discussion" (*Ibid.*, 586). Absolutely no parley—was it worth the name of diplomacy?

Other sources say that when Nehru sent an Indian Delegation headed by N. Raghavan to the Conference, Nehru's directive to them contained some surprise if we look back at it. It says that "We should not raise this (frontier) question. If the Chinese raise it, we should express our surprise and point out that this is a settled issue...there has never been any reference to this frontier issue and it is surprising that this should be brought up now" (SWJN-2, 24-598-9). India's Ambassador K.M. Panikkar went even further and said that if the Chinese side wants to take up the frontier issue "the Indian delegation could walk out of the conference and break off the negotiations" (*Ibid.*, 598fn3).

If the Indian side had so wanted, they could have concluded the border question under the terms favourable to them at this time. But they, and especially Nehru, had no such wishes. It is as if they kept their determination to themselves, and believed what the Chinese told them as to the maps. Nehru wrote a Note to the Secretary-General and Foreign Secretary in the External Affairs Ministry the next year

(1954) in which he said that India's frontier "should be considered a firm and definite one which is not open to discussion with anybody" (SWJN-2, 26-481-4). This was only a few days after the above Joint Statement had been issued. After about two more years, on 6 May 1956, he wrote a Note to Krishna Menon in which he said that "The Tibet frontier ran along the McMahon Line and we consider it a firm frontier…All that they have said is that the old maps are not reliable." (SWJN-2, 33-475-7). It was as if Menon was a Deputy Foreign Minister.

When it comes to the question of how long the areas south of the McMahon Line had been under the Indian administration, however, we see Nehru making one important admission. Late in 1953 he was writing on an ambush by the local tribal people of the Indian military in the NEFA, "not far from our Tibetan border", and said, "This place is far in the interior and not easy of access. It has been and is still unadministered territory. We are gradually spreading out our administration there" (LCM, 3-435).

Without taking sides in the border dispute, would it be less than fair to Nehru to say that here he was not able to show that the area had belonged to India rather than having been no man's land? What Nehru said here would coincide with the advance of the Indian power to Tawang in 1951, or the British taking the Tawang Tract a few years before, mentioned earlier in this chapter.

Several years afterwards, after the Dalai Lama had fled into India, and the two armed clashes occurred between India and China, all in 1959, Nehru was writing on the NEFA as, for example, follows. "We had a few checkposts but they were not actually on the border…a great part of this territory, which is largely uninhabited, had no checkposts or border forces…This was indeed almost the first attempt for this kind of investigation and survey as previously all these vast areas had been rather neglected and ignored because of the great difficulty of access and also because no danger was apprehended there" (LCM, 5-306). Where is the solid evidence that these areas have been part of the Indian territory, and what is the use of claiming that these areas belong to India, let alone shedding blood for their sake?

Nehru's China Visit

After Zhou's India visit in June 1954, which confirmed the *Panchsheel* principles, Nehru made a visit to China and Vietnam. He wrote a long Note on his visit. Only two bureaucrats are mentioned there who accompanied him, N.R. Pillai, Secretary General from the External Affairs Ministry, and N. Raghavan, India's Ambassador to China (LCM, 4-76). Here also Nehru was seen not training politicians of the next generation. Was he so keen to manage everything himself? Did he not like the upcoming of young people?

Concerning the maps, Nehru said to Zhou during his visit that "we were not much concerned about this matter because our boundaries were quite clear and were not a matter for argument" (LCM, 4-82). He did not have to be so appeasing. But at the same time it may be said that Nehru had refused in advance to talk about the border issue. Zhou did not seem to bother about Nehru's attitude either because Nehru writes that "Premier Chou replied that these maps were old ones and China had not done any surveying to draw new maps" (*Ibid.*). It was a time when China was not expanding and there were no other lingering problems between India and China. The Sino-Pakistani relations had not become so close by this time either. China and Pakistan started contacting at the Bandung Conference of 1955.[15] Although speaking with hindsight, it must be said that India missed an opportunity, which may not have been the only one but the best one, to settle the border problem with China.

A few years afterwards, however, Zhou began to say that the border of the two countries had not been officially determined. Probably his second visit to India and the series of talks he had with Nehru on 31 December, 1956 to 1 January, 1957 were the first such occasion. Zhou said on the McMahon Line then that "Now, that it is an accomplished fact, we should accept it. So, although, the question is still undecided and it is unfair to us, still we feel that there is no better way than to recognize this Line...the question can be solved and we think it should be solved early" (SWJN-2, 36-583-603). This is in the same tone as Guha has interpreted some of Zhou's later correspondence and statements. Nehru did not respond to it on this occasion. But Nehru, referring to the McMahon Line in his letter to Zhou on 14 December, 1958, wanted to know if "you proposed to recognize this border with India also" during his previous visit to India in 1956-57 (SWJN-2, 46-704). This, too, was before Zhou's letters of 1959 that Guha mentioned. Zhou was not entirely in favour of making the McMahon

Line the border, but it seems he was ready to make that compromise. Unfortunately, however, Nehru was not prepared to grasp that hand. This was probably the last chance to do so in peaceful and quiet circumstances. China's stance began becoming harder, as India's was hard from the beginning.

The Year 1959

Then came a letter from Zhou En-lai to Nehru dated 23 January, 1959. It was a reply to Nehru's of December the previous year, but did not directly give an answer to what Nehru was asking. It said that, "the Sino-Indian boundary has never been formally delimitated", therefore 'border disputes do exist', but they want "to take a more or less realistic attitude towards the McMahon Line". His proposal, therefore, was "as a provisional measure, the two sides temporarily maintain the *status quo*". Zhou also said that the Chinese did not discuss it in the 1954 Tibet Conference as their study of the problem was not complete (SWJN-2, 47- 557-60).

Nehru's reply went on 22 March, 1959. He said that the traditional frontier was the watershed, which was fortified by international agreements. As the examples of the latter he mentioned the Treaties of 1842 and 1847 for Ladakh in the Western Sector. He also mentioned the McMahon Line for the Eastern Sector.

Very soon the Dalai Lama sought asylum in India. A telegram from G. Parthasarathi, India's Ambassador to China, to Nehru dated 3 May, 1959 after the asylum was very serious. It told Nehru that the anti-Indian campaign in China was now very intense, the issues raised go beyond Tibet and the frontier is the most important, they say that the Tibetan rebellion was the joint work of the Indian reactionaries and the British imperialists. It also said that he is at the moment unable to talk to the Chinese officials. Formally Zhou En-lai used to come and brief him for at least 10 minutes about the current problems, the Ambassador presumably meaning receptions and other gatherings, but it was not so in the past several meetings, and it is no use talking to other Chinese officials except Zhou (SWJN-2, 48- 601-3).

Then came Zhou's 8 September letter, his first after the Dalai Lama's asylum, which says that "Indians kept missing clues in the Chinese correspondence that not all the territory China might *theoretically* have a claim to would *actually* be claimed by them. Further clues that China might be flexible in the North East in return for Indian flexibility in the North West was also ignored." It should be noticed that this letter came before the two letters that Guha discussed in the above. We may say that China was keen to negotiate, at least at this moment, but not India.

Zhou's letter, however, used some rigid words concerning the border issue. It says that Zhou had read Nehru's letter carefully, and there is 'a fundamental difference' in approach between the two countries, and specifically mentions four points from the Chinese side. (1) The boundary has not been delimited. The McMahon Line is 'decidedly illegal'. 90,000 square kilometres of the Chinese territory has been under the Indian occupation, and the Indian forces have come up to the Line around 1951. (2) But the Chinese forces have never crossed the Line. (3) When the Indian forces attacked Migyitun from Longju, it became "the first instance of armed clash along the Sino-Indian border". (4) The Chinese 'guard units' are stationed in the south-east Tibet in order to suppress rebellion.

Meanwhile the Education Minister Maulana Azad passed away in 1958, which, in Zachariah's view, was "making Nehru the last representative of the giants of the nationalist movement left in government."[16] In that government, as Krishna Menon recalled, "there was seldom a major debate in Cabinet because of everyone's great respect for Nehru."[17] Nehru himself reportedly told a foreign scientist in 1954 that "Most of my Ministers are reactionary and scoundrels...."[18]

In reply to Zhou En-lai's letter of 8 September, 1959, Nehru on 26 September, categorically rejected China's claim over 40,000 square miles of Indian territory based on old Chinese maps (LCM, 5-285fn11). Nehru described the Chinese claim thus, "This is a demand for considerable areas, more especially in the N.E.F.A. All this means the Chinese want to come down on this side of the Himalayan barrier" (*Ibid.*, 288): Actually Nehru's reply included 29 items. Some of them are as follows. (1) When he got Chou's 23 January letter he had no idea China would claim 40,000 square miles of the Indian territory. (2) The Chinese army conquered Longju on the Indian side of the Line. (9) The whole of Aksai Chin belongs to India. Kuen Lun is its northern periphery. (13) China initialed both the Convention and the Map at Simla. Therefore, they are binding on China also. (15) The tribes inhabiting south of the Line are of the same ethnic stock as those inhabiting other parts of Assam, and not Tibetans. Owing to the several arrangements of the nineteenth century the Indian administration has gradually infiltrated them and that is the basis of the Line. (20) The Chinese have crossed the Line, at Kinzemane and Longju. (21) In the West also the Chinese attacked Spanggrur. (28) He wants to maintain the *status quo*. For that the traditional frontier should be observed.

There occurred two armed clashes in that year, one each on the NEFA, where the Indian post of Longju was "outflanked and overwhelmed" (*Ibid.*, 301fn2) in August, and in eastern Ladakh, "on the other side of the main Himalayan range" (*Ibid.*, 304), where "Chinese armed guards attacked an Indian patrol in the neighbourhood of Kongka Pass" in October (*Ibid.*, 303fn1).

Both the Governments were busily engaged with the border question from September onwards in that year 1959. First, there was a Note by the Chinese Ministry of Foreign Affairs to the Indian Ambassador Parthasarathi of 1 September. It said that Indian forces occupied Longju in the East, thus causing the first armed clash in the conflict. The place belongs to China even under the McMahon Line which, China has not accepted (SWJN-2, 52-304-7). Then followed Zhou's letter of 8 September to Nehru, already mentioned, in reply to the latter's of 22 March. It claims that the McMahon Line had been signed in Delhi in secret in 1914, China does not recognize it, and the Indian forces came up to the south of this Line only in 1951 (*Ibid.*, 309-316), meaning that it had not been historically a part of India.

Zhou's letter of 8 September was 'markedly less cordial' than the previous one, which again stressed that the border had never been fixed, and in the East India had illegally occupied the 56,000 square miles of Chinese territory between the McMahon Line and the Himalayan foot-hills. In the West it had been customary to regard Aksai Chin as a Chinese territory. India thought, correctly, that China was claiming the whole of NEFA.[19]

In his reply to Zhou on 26 September, Nehru wrote that Longju is "on our side of the McMahon Line", and so is Khinzemane which China claims and has occupied. The McMahon Line is "the customary boundary", and the boundary East of Bhutan is by this Line. It was

China which disrupted the *status quo* by building a road in Aksai Chin which belongs to India (SWJN-2, 52- 216-231).

Zhou wrote back to say, on 7 November, that there was again a clash in the Chinese territory south of the Kongka Pass in the Western sector. This was the second such clash. He proposed that both sides would retreat by 20 km each from the McMahon Line in the East and the line of 'actual control' in the West, his first such proposal for mutual withdrawal, thus making a 40-km-wide neutral zone. It is difficult to say which side would benefit more from this proposal. But, if put into effect, there would have been no 1962.

But, it was not to be, because Nehru made a counter proposal on 16 November, which was that each would withdraw to the line claimed by the other side. It also claimed that 'the entire territory' up to the Line belonged to India, and Longju and Khinzemani were both on the Indian side of the Line (SWJN-2, 54- 492-8). This proposal was apparently impossible to put into practice. Zhou said in his reply of 17 December that his was the only possible proposal in this case, India's was 'unfair', and in fact the area south of the McMahon Line "not long ago, was still under the jurisdiction of the local Government of the Tibetan region of China" (SWJN-2, 55-467-474). The above two letters by Zhou were the ones mentioned by Guha.

On the general situation in China around this time Odd Arne Westad writes in his *Restless Empire* that the Great Leap Forward Policy in China, started from 1958, brought a great damage to her economy and the people's life. First deaths were reported from the winter of 1958 to 1959, and by the time it was over in 1961, 45 million were presumed to be dead. Moreover, some new 'major purge' got in preparation already in 1965.[20]

On 26 December, toward the end of 1959, Ministry of Foreign Affairs of China put three questions to the Embassy of India in China. These were,

Question I. Has the Sino-Indian Boundary been Formally Delimited?

Question II. Where is the Traditional Customary Sino-Indian Boundary Line?

Question III. What is the Proper Way to Settle the Sino-Indian Boundary Dispute?

After deploying their own argument at considerable length, the Chinese concluded that the boundary has never been delimited, therefore, it is necessary to solve the problem by negotiations, and for both to withdraw by 20 km till then (SWJN-2, 56-398-423).

The 1960 Nehru-Zhou Summit

The Government of India sent its own Note in reply to the above on 12 February, 1960 to the Chinese Government. It consists of 42 items. The salient points are as follows:

> No. 4. China claimed a vast territory of India for the first time on 8 September, 1959. This was the beginning of the dispute.
> No. 15. The Indian maps of the border are based on 'the main watershed'.
> No. 23. The Chinese theory that the area south of the traditional boundary east of Bhutan has been a part of China is wrong.
> No. 25. Tawang and Walong are included in such an area. But 'Tawang was never a part of Tibet'.
> No. 31. China always questions the validity of the Indo-Tibetan Treaty of 1914. But at that time all the three delegations exchanged their credentials on an equal footing.
> No. 32. The Chinese Delegate also signed on 27 April, 1914 what is shown on the map as the Indo-Tibetan boundary. China never protested.
> No. 33. That is the McMahon Line.
> No. 35. The Prime Minister of India declared publicly that India stood by the McMahon Line in 1950 (SWJN-2, 57-501-15), implying that China had never denied it since then.

It was in such a rather cold and hostile atmosphere in Delhi that Zhou arrived in April end of that year for one more, the last, and a disastrous summit with Nehru.

Nehru's attitude was rigid throughout. He wrote, for example, in his memo that the border was "not open to discussion with anybody".[21] He had brought the Indian people to believe that the Indian military was able to face the Chinese Army, so that the military measure was the only one left for tackling China now.[22] He actually believed till the last that India would defeat China.[23] Unfortunately, he was not serious on getting precise military information on the two forces facing each other.

Zhou came to India and had long talks with Nehru and others for the last time in April 1960. The two had altogether seven meetings on this occasion. Broadly their talks were as follows.

The first meeting was held for two hours on 20 April, 1960.

Nehru said that in September the previous year China for the first time said that their maps were correctly depicting her territory. China had made no such comment for years till then. Also, he did not agree that the whole boundary was undefined. It is defined by the watershed.

Zhou said that "The activities of Dalai Lama and his followers have far exceeded the limits of political asylum."

The second meeting was held for two hours on the same day.

Zhou asked if first of all the boundary had been delimited in terms of latitude and longitude. For the maps there should be a survey. The eastern sector (the McMahon Line) is the result of the secret exchange of notes between Britain and Tibet. China, therefore, will not recognize it, but will not cross it also. The south of the Line is Tibet. In the western sector India for the first time in 1959 included Aksai Chin as its new territorial claim. It is a part of China's Sinkiang Province.

The third meeting was held for two and a half hours on 21 April.

Nehru said that from his own experience of visiting the area, the whole of Aksai Chin cannot be a part of China. China has not replied to India on Aksai Chin, Kongka Pass and Longju.

Zhou said that there is a dispute in the Eastern Sector but there is no such thing in the Western Sector though China has built a road in Aksai Chin.

The fourth meeting was held for three hours on 22 April.

Zhou made a detailed presentation on the Facts, the Common Ground, and New Proposals. As regards the Facts, Zhou said that in the Eastern Sector "the traditional and customary line" lies south of the McMahon Line. The British from 1942 during the Second World War shifted the Line northward. After independence India expanded her administrative apparatus up to the present Line by 1954. The Line was originally the boundary of Inner and Outer Tibet. Therefore, it is not suitable to be taken up in a discussion of this sort, but India brought it in and made it complicated. China will not accept the argument. Can there be no solution of the matter? No, that is not so. Though the PRC does not recognize it, they will not cross it, and in the two or three places where India crossed it China stands for the maintenance of the *status quo*. Zhou said concerning the Western Sector that the Karakoram Range, which is up to Kongka Pass is the border of Sinkiang and Ladakh, and it lies to the west of the Kuen Lun, which is the border of Sinkiang and Tibet. These areas were undefined till 1954.

As regards the Common Ground, Zhou said that in the East the border is not defined and we must discuss it. In the West China recognizes 'a traditional customary line', but since India thinks it should be more to the east some common understanding is necessary. A line of actual control at present is the McMahon Line in the East and the Karakoram and the Kongka Pass in the West. The watershed may not necessarily be the only standard. Both should not claim an area over which they have no administrative control at present, as India is doing in the West. And national feelings, for example spiritual value attached to particular mountains, should be respected.

(We will skip over Zhou's New Proposals)

The fifth meeting was held for three and a quarter hours on 23 April.

Nehru pointed out that it was only a short while before 1957 that China entered North Aksai Chin.

Zhou contradicted it by saying that, among others, the Karakoram watershed is the boundary in the region, and north of Aksai Chin is already in Sinkiang.

The sixth meeting was held for three and a quarter hours on 24 April.

Zhou said that Aksai Chin was in Sinkiang for a long time, and Sinkiang has been in China for 200 years.

Nehru: Except the eastern part where China built a road, the rest of Aksai Chin had been under China for only a year or a year and a half, has it not?

Zhou: The north and the east of the Karakoram watershed belong to Sinkiang.

Nehru: "For generations there has been no sign of Chinese or Tibetans in the eastern and southern parts of Ladakh. This is a basic thing."

Zhou: It may be so from the administrative point of view. But the Chinese jurisdiction has been there. Aksai Chin has been under Khotan in Sinkiang. The boundary was undelimited, but India drew a line both in the East and the West in 1954.

The seventh and the last meeting was held for one hour and three quarters on 25 April. The draft communique of both sides was discussed and a joint communique was issued, saying that the talks had not led to resolving the differences but they would be examined by the officials of both the countries.

It was followed by Zhou's Press Conference extending for two and a quarter hours. He said two important things then. He said he hoped that India would take the same policy in the Western Sector as China is taking in the Eastern Sector. This must be what Guha has pointed out. Zhou at the same time threatened that if India claims Aksai Chin, China would demand the withdrawal of India from the area sandwiched by the two boundary lines drawn on the Chinese map and the Indian map.

Officials' Work

The officials of the two countries did their work. As far as India was concerned, *Report of the Officials of the Governments of India and the People's Republic of China on the Boundary Question*, signed in Rangoon, one of the three places together with Beijing and Delhi where the officials from both sides had met, on 12 December, 1960, was placed in the Lok Sabha on 14 February, 1961. The Report constitutes a full-sized book of about 600 pages as Volume 66 *Supplement* in the SWJN-2, as separate from Volume 66, and was published on the same day. We will call it the *Supplement* here. It is a single book but is actually what has bound together the report by the Indian side and the report by the Chinese side. We will see what it says on the Indo-Chinese boundary issue with somewhat more emphasis on the Indian report.

The Indian side was headed by Jagat S. Mehta, a Joint Secretary in the Ministry of External Affairs, with S. Gopal as his deputy who was Director, the Historical Division of the Ministry. Gopal writes in the Preface to Vol. 1 of his biography of Nehru that "I saw him almost everyday" from April 1959 to December 1962. No other names are mentioned. Mehta says that the verbatim record of the whole of the three series of the sessions amounting to 3,000 pages exists, but it is "available only for reference in the Ministry".

At the beginning we come across a section called "Salient Points of the Indian Summary". It consists of seven short excerpts. Skipping over (1) and (6), it is mentioned in (2) that at the sessions of the officials both sides exchanged their own maps of the areas on which they are going to give their evidence that those areas belong to them. It also says that the Chinese maps were 'much smaller'. (3) Then at the sessions the evidence and the "point to point description of the boundary" were given, and questions and answers followed. The description by the Chinese side was 'much vaguer' and they could not answer many of the questions asked by the Indian side. This is because they had not been in control of the southern parts of Tibet and Sinkiang till recently. (4) The number of items provided by the Indian side was 650, whereas that by China was only 245. (5) Against the Chinese argument that India had not been aware of the road building in Aksai Chin, and therefore, it was not part of India, the Indian side replied that 'trespass' does not constitute 'legitimate title'. (7) This is a 'Conclusion', which are the excerpts of the whole report. We will see it in more detail later. Mehta, however, writes something significant here. He says that this part has been written by himself, and is the most important part of the whole report. Before taking off to Rangoon for the final series of discussion, he and Gopal showed the draft of it, about 80 pages, to Nehru, who took about two hours to read it 'carefully' and 'approved'. So, the whole report can be said closely to reflect Nehru's thinking.

Then we come to a group of six points which are said to have escaped the critics' eyes thus far. The author has taken it to mean that those are considered to be either new points or points not fully discussed thus far. They are as follows: (1) There is 'triple coincidence' in the Indian boundary, meaning traditional, natural, and the McMahon Line. (2) Even if you discard the whole of the Indian evidence, the Chinese evidence alone will testify the correctness of the Indian view. (3) On the Eastern Sector China has not given any evidence covering the whole area. On the other hand "Our evidence in the Western Sector was comparatively meagre", but there is nothing to show that it is a part of Sinkiang. China has not controlled the area south of the Kuen Lun Range by 1950s. (4) The status of Tibet is the most difficult question. (5) May be skipped over. And (6) says that "The facts, therefore, demand respect for this boundary defined by Nature, confirmed by history and sanctioned by the laws of nation".

The Indian side has added here that the 'positive support' to the Chinese claim is 'truly meagre'. S. Gopal also writes here that the Chinese evidence is 'scanty', and moreover, they have 'little precise knowledge' on the border area.

We now come to the main Indian report. It consists of four parts. We will summarize I here, skip over II and III, and describe in more detail the content of IV, the last part, titled Conclusion, which had been seen and approved by Nehru in its draft stage as we saw before.

I. Location and Natural Features of the Boundary

Here the Indian side gave their own description of the boundary as starting from the trijunction of India, China and Afghanistan, going over the Khunjerab and other passes which are on the watershed, to the Karakoram Pass, crossing the Indus five miles south east of Demchok, and ultimately leading to the trijunction of India, Nepal and Tibet. Thus in the Indian view the boundary was delimited. The Chinese side, however, while giving their own "Location and Terrain Features of the Traditional Customary Sino-Indian boundary line", took the stand that it was not. In the discussion concerning the two contradictory concepts of the boundary line, China did not give reply to half of the questions asked by the Indian side, and much of the reply they gave was incomplete. India answered all the questions China asked, except one.

One important point India raised in supporting their boundary concept was the watershed. They said, "That the watershed principle was a valid and legitimate one in determining boundaries had been recognized in all parts of the world, and it was incorrect to state, as the Chinese side had done, that it was a British concept." Further, they said that in the Eastern Sector the difference between what China claimed and the traditional customary boundary along the watershed was great. As a consequence more than 30,000 square miles are in dispute. This is because China claims that the traditional and customary line was the southern foothills of the Himalayas. In the Middle Sector as well as Nepal, Sikkim, Bhutan and Burma the Himalayan watershed is considered to be the boundary (*Supplement*, 76-7).

II. Traditional and Customary Basis of the Sino-Indian Boundary in the Western Sector.

III. Basis of the Indian Alignment in Administration and Jurisdiction.

These two sub-sections may be safely skipped over here.

Conclusion

This is the crux of the Indian viewpoint without which the *Supplement* would be incomplete and not definitive. Nehru read its draft in about 80 pages. It now occupies 55 pages, pp. 271 to 325, in the *Supplement*, which is from pp. 233 to 287 of the original report as is printed in the book.

It is divided into 15 sub-sections each under an alphabetical letter from A to O. In the beginning it says that "the true traditional boundary" is what India is claiming. There are two alignments facing each other. That is the fact. But which one is "the true traditional boundary"? It is India's. "The majestic arc of the Kuen Lun and the Great Himalayan Ranges" are the boundary.

A. *Introduction*: We may skip over this.

B. *Geographical Facts and Principles*: India has depended on her maps of one million to one, but Chinese maps were one and a half million to one. The Indian side answered all the 60 or so questions asked by the Chinese side. But China replied only about half of the 120 or so questions by India. The Chinese description was vague, and contained few specific co-ordinates. It seems China had not conducted surveys on their border areas and was, therefore, ignorant of them. Actually, the Chinese side did not like incorporating their own description and their own replies to the Indian questions into this report. India questioned about Longju or Khinzemane (both in the Eastern Sector) in detail. But they were told by the Chinese that the Indian questions were 'minute and trifling', meaning embarrassing to them. In India's view the natural dividing line was by tradition and custom, and conforms to the watershed. For the Chinese the watershed sometimes did not. It was when they moved their boundary toward the Indian side and away from the watershed. The whole boundary in southern China is "the same continuing Himalayan watershed" and not its foothills.

Incidentally, the Chinese side complained the way India counted the number of their questions and answers. They said, "In listing the questions and answers of the two sides...the Indian side...often only listed as one answer for the answers actually given by the Chinese side to two or more questions put forward by the Indian side (while it often listed one of the own questions as two or even three questions), thereby greatly increasing the number of the questions raised by the Indian side and reducing that of the answers given by the Chinese side" (*Supplement*, 576).

C. *Documentary Evidence*: The number of the Indian evidence is much more than the Chinese evidence.

D. *The Indian Evidence*: The Western Sector. It was at the end of the nineteenth century that Sinkiang expanded to Kuen Lun. "This made it clear that the Aksai Chin plateau and the Lingji Tang plains were never a part of China." At the same time some police check posts of the Kashmir Government were to be seen in northern Aksai Chin in 1865. On the inhabited areas to the south, like Demchok, there exists a record of regular administration.

The Middle Sector: This part is to be skipped over.

The Eastern Sector: Here 'disinterested travellers', or 'British travellers', have expressed their view that the Himalaya was the limit of Tibet. So, did the Chinese maps. The areas between the Himalayan foothills and its main range were always under the Indian rule.

E. *The McMahon Line*: This line as the traditional boundary was formalized by the exchange of letters between India and Tibet. At the time Tibet was authorized to conclude treaties. China had recognized it, and was aware of the formalization. At the moment the Government of India deals with the Tibetan border only through the Chinese Government. But historically it was different.

At Simla the Chinese Government dealt with the Tibetan representatives on an equal footing. China and Tibet had been cut apart completely because of the Chinese Revolution of 1911. What China refused to sign was the boundary of Inner Tibet and Outer Tibet. The Red Line drawn on the Convention Map and formalized between India and Tibet was not commented upon by China. The areas below that Line cannot but be part of India. In fact most of the Chinese evidence is from Tibetan sources.

F. *Maps and Surveys*: Many of the maps India has produced for discussion are from China and other places, which testifies the validity of the Indian view. The first survey of Aksai Chin was done by the British about 20 years after Kashmir came under the Raj. China has not been able to produce "a single published official Chinese map" concerning the boundary of the land they claim that they have ruled for centuries. As against the 13 Indian official maps China produced, the reverse was 36.

The official surveys by India of Aksai Chin, Lingzi Tang, and Chang Chenno were coming out from 1863 onwards. It was not the result of what the Chinese side called 'sneaking'. On the other hand China has failed to produce a single such survey.

G. *Meagre Contents of the Chinese case*: The population inhabiting the 32,000 square miles China claims in the Eastern Sector is not Buddhist as they say but 'tribal people'. The Indian evidence regarding them includes "revenue settlements, land taxes, official tours and other aspects of general administration". On the other hand China has offered "no evidence of any revenue collection, of survey operation, of acquaintance with the cultivated lower valleys or of construction of public wells in the inhabited areas."

On the Western Sector, the Chinese claims are supported by illegal occupation (of Aksai Chin). Their own evidence and maps show that Sinkiang had not expanded to the south of the Kuen Lun range.

H. *Deficiencies and Contradictions in the Chinese Evidence*: There are several sub-sections here. In sub-section (ii), on 'unsupported assertions', the Chinese claim, for instance, that the people of Sinkiang were visiting Aksai Chin for 'salt-mining, pasturing, trading', but without any evidence. To this the Indian side provided evidence that it was actually the people of Ladakh. In (iii) the Indian side pointed out that the Chinese had not put any border marks at places like Kongka Pass.

In (vi) on the inconsistencies in the Chinese evidence, it is said that Ladakh and Tibet are of equal status and the former is not a part of the latter. It is further said that "The contradictions in the Chinese case are so numerous, and their implications are so serious and far-reaching that they serve to disintegrate the Chinese evidence and position."

I. *Chinese Comments on Indian Evidence*: The Chinese by and large have given no specific comments on the Indian evidence. At the same time they like to ignore the Indian evidence, which has surprised the

Indian side. They tend to turn down whatever ideas they do not like by calling them 'imperialist'. But they could not show a single such example of imperial fabrication. They have only made profit by making use of the term.

J. *Chinese Report*: This may be safely skipped over.

K. *West of the Karakoram Pass*: The Chinese officials prefer not to discuss this area as in their view it comes outside their mandate. The Indian side suspects that this attitude amounts to the refusal to recognize the accession of Jammu & Kashmir to India.

L. *China had never Affirmed the Boundary*: The Government of India came to know the Chinese claim for the first time in September 1959. It was five years since the Indian Government first took up the issue with the Chinese Government. During these years India had only known the various Chinese maps. They involved a disputed area of 50,000 square miles.

The note by the Chinese Government of 26 December, 1959 says that it was Nehru himself who took up the maps with Zhou in 1954. In the Chinese reply of 3 November, 1958 to the Indian Government's note of 21 August of the same year, China was still talking of the errors of the maps. Zhou's reply of 23 January, 1959 to Nehru's letter of 14 December, 1958 said the same thing. When an Indian was apprehended in Aksai Chin in September 1958, the Chinese sent a letter dated 3 November, of the same date as the one above, that the area was a part of China, in reply to an Indian letter of the previous month.

From these it may be said that "the Chinese claims are of very recent origin", and they put those claims "on suitable occasions".

M. *The Chinese evidence testifies India's correctness*: Even without all the Indian evidence, the Chinese evidence will prove India to be correct. In the Western Sector, the southernmost end of Sinkiang was in Kuen Lun or still to the north. The northernmost part of Kashmir was in Kuen Lun and it included Aksai Chin. According to the Chinese material, Ladakh was independent till it was merged with the Mughal Empire, and the Chinese theory that it was a part of Tibet till the nineteenth century collapses. Moreover the kings of Ladakh and Tibet made peace in 1684, meaning that there was a boundary between the two. The Karakoram Pass goes through Ladakh and therefore, cannot be that boundary.

In the Eastern Sector, in Tawang there was Indian jurisdiction early in the nineteenth century. Also the area south of the Himalaya was transferred from the Ahom to the Raj in the nineteenth century.

Therefore, even depending on the Chinese material, the boundary runs through Kuen Lun Range, near Demchok, near Kanirik, across the Shipki Pass, above Barahoti and to the McMahon Line. The Indian administration had reached this line.

N. *Indian Boundary is already delimited*: (i) Therefore, the boundary is already valid, and does not need more definition. But the Chinese are saying that, on one hand, the present line is too broad and approximate, but, on the other hand, the line they have drawn is precise and clear. (ii) To be skipped over. (iii) There are historical precedents that small disputes put the validity of the whole frontiers in bold relief. The Sino-Burmese treaty has affirmed that the traditional boundary based on the Himalayan watershed does exist and it conforms to the McMahon Line. (iv) Therefore, we need no delimitation specifically. The Chinese side is also saying the same thing, which is that "a traditional line was so clear that it needed no delimitation" and it "requires no further definition". It is something optional.

O. *Conclusion*: So, which alignment is the 'true traditional boundary'? This is the 'crux'.

We have shown rather a long summary of the Indian part of the *Supplement*. The three series of talks did very little to narrow the gap in perception between the two countries. The negotiations stopped there. They were now facing a break-down. That was what the SWJN-2 has led us to believe by up to its Volume 70 as of October 2017.

A Discussion in the Lok Sabha

However, the Library of the Institute of Developing Economies, Japan, with the help of a bookshop in Gurgaon, has acquired six new volumes, Volumes 71-76, of the SWJN more recently, and the author has hurriedly glanced over them. 74 to 76 have been published in 2018.

Out of these Volumes the documents concerning the Belgrade Conference, the First Non-Aligned Summit, of 1961, are most important, especially in the field of Nehru's Foreign Policy. There is no particularly important single document or speech concerning his

China policy. But there are several significant Parliamentary debates on the Indo-Chinese questions, and the Discussion on the Chinese Incursions in the Lok Sabha on 5 December, 1961 in Volume 73 is more important among them, as it was a long one, some prominent Opposition Members often interrupted, but ultimately Nehru did most of the talking while giving away his own conviction (SWJN-2, 73-564-586).

There were five major points which came up in the Discussion.

One. A reply came from the Chinese Government, dated 30 November, which, as Nehru said, 'of course, as usual, denied and repudiated the various charges that we had made against them'.

Two. In spite of that, however, Nehru himself "laid the greatest stress on the importance of this matter to India, not only in the present but in the future, and I said this problem in some shape or other might pursue us for a generation or more, and we could not consider it lightly or superficially. What happens on our border is a basic problem, it is a problem of historic importance. So that nobody can charge me with not attaching enough importance to it."

Three. Therefore to Nehru the problem is the 'vacation of aggression'. He continued. 'How should we get that vacated?' Always through peaceful methods. Apart from peaceful methods, there are pressures short of war and then there is war.

Now, I am free to confess to this House that my whole soul reacts against the idea of war anywhere. This is the training I have received throughout my life and I cannot easily get rid of it at the age of 72.

"...We are friendly with every country in the world including China, but we will fight China if necessary. That is the whole lesson that I have been taught during the last 40 or 50 years of my life by Gandhiji and others: always to be friendly and never to give in."

Four. On Tibet. When N.G. Ranga criticized Nehru by saying that 'you allowed the Chinese to come there and you made no arrangements', Nehru's reply was that 'I really cannot understand how else or what other policy we could have adopted...I am completely unrepentant about the policy we adopted towards Tibet.'

Five. General attitude to China. Nehru also said that 'China has not lived up to' the principles of Panchsheel. But nevertheless India has voted for China's seat in the UN as late as 'even last year'.

These five were all important points and worth discussing. They were, however, discussed here only in abstract terms. In other words they were not discussed in concrete terms from the point of view of how Nehru and his Government were handling those issues, particularly the all-important Indo-Chinese border issue. Nehru on his own did not frankly tell the Members what his policy was and where the difficulty lay. Similarly the Members did not raise these detailed questions. It is all the more surprising as December 1961 was on the eve of the fatal year 1962, and Nehru's Forward Policy had already been introduced on the ground.

Would it be too harsh to say that the Parliament, with all its galaxy of eminent speakers, was putting so much confidence in Nehru that it failed to give an alternative not only to itself but to the nation as a whole?

Subimal Dutt on Nehru

At the end of this Chapter we will consult an Indian diplomat's memoir, so that we will look at the subject matter of this Chapter from a little different angle. It is called *With Nehru in the Foreign Office*, by Subimal Dutt who was officially in touch with Nehru for 15 years, including 12 years of 'close daily contact'. He finally resigned as Foreign Secretary and got appointed as Ambassador to the USSR in April 1961.

During these years Dutt naturally had a busy contact with China under Nehru. The PRC declared on the New Year's Day 1950 that it will liberate Tibet, and the latter wanted help from India and other countries. According to him, Britain and Tibet conferred and produced the McMahon Line, a Red line on the map, on which all the three parties concerned including China put their signature. But there was no subsequent claim by China regarding the Line.

The official maps of China claimed about 32,000 square miles in the Eastern Sector, 10,000 to 14,000 in the Western Sector and several hundred in the Central Sector of the Indian territory, but none of these is under their administration.

Nehru talked to Zhou on these maps during his China visit in 1954. But when Zhou said that the maps were old ones, "Nehru did not press the point."[24] When Zhou visited India for the second time at the end of 1956, he said that China studied the McMahon Line in connection with the Sino-Burmese relations, the Line was certainly not fair, but the PRC should accept it as it is there already and the friendship of India and Burma is important to China. This was before what Guha was referring to. But he wrote to Nehru at the end of January 1959 that he had not said that China would accept the Line, but some suitable boundary would be found.

When Zhou came for the last time in April 1960, "Nehru was worried by the extremely rigid attitude of the Chinese Premier." Zhou said at his midnight Press Conference that "As China was prepared to accommodate the Indian point of view in the Eastern Sector, India should accommodate China in the western sector...". This is what Guha has talked about. But, Nehru firmly said when seeing Zhou off at the Delhi Airport the next morning that "there could be no question of a barter".[25] We may say that Zhou was not entertaining the idea of a war with India at this time, as his proposal did not necessarily imply a collision course with India. But what about Nehru? Would it be less than fair to him to say that in all probability it must have occurred to him at this time that it meant a collision course with the PRC to reject all ideas of a barter? Otherwise what possible scenario was he ever able to picture before him if he brushed aside a barter? Or did it never occur to him that the Chinese would resort to their arms, even in case India would?

Here what Han Suyin has written on India's or rather Nehru's conviction may be at least of some value. She says, "Zhou had already settled or was in the process of settling similar undefined border problems with Burma, with Nepal and Pakistan. India was now being lauded—and courted—by both the United States and the USSR, and was receiving generous aid from both. Nehru had no reason to settle the Chinese border problem. "I tried everything I could, but I could not move Nehru at all", Zhou said."[26] Her analysis may be useful in understanding the 'map or no map' policy.

A few years ago it could have been different as several outstanding persons were still there, if not Sardar Patel. But now, as Dutt was writing, "The entire Cabinet was united in its opposition to any settlement on the basis of barter." The atmosphere in Delhi to receive Zhou, possibly the most important guest India might receive at this time in her own national interest, had definitely cooled down compared to the previous two or three occasions judging from the cartoons in the newspapers or the *Shankar's Weekly* at this time, and astonishingly so, and was very much unfit for welcoming Zhou and having a heart-to-heart talk. The atmosphere was overwhelmingly that the Chinese have deceived India, and cannot be trusted. It was no less intense in the Lok Sabha, and it is natural that Nehru was under heavy constraint by it.

Dutt also makes some comments on the Chinese attitude. He said, "the Chinese definitely revised their attitude to India" after the Dalai Lama's visit to India by invitation in November to December 1956. They must have begun to see him as a possible enemy from then on. He also referred to The *People's Daily*, which carried two articles on India, "The Tibetan Revolution and Nehru's Philosophy", and Again on Nehru's Philosophy", in 6 May, 1959 and 27 October, 1962, respectively, which were critical of Nehru.

Out of the two, the first one was soft and polite. But it still condemned Nehru as having called the rebellion in Tibet as a nationalist revolution and its putting down as a tragedy which were all baseless. Nehru had made such a speech in the Lok Sabha seven times already. It comes out of the dual character of the India's big bourgeoisie, it says.

The second, however, was no longer soft or polite. It said that India came on an all-out offensive against China on 20 October, 1962. They are the representatives of the big bourgeoisie and big landlords. India is depending more and more on foreign aid. In the Eastern Sector India has occupied up to the McMahon Line, and at some places beyond that. In the Central Sector they have taken 2,000 square kilometres, and in the West they are claiming the land under the Chinese administration. The Malaviya Committee that has visited China was impressed by the land reform there. But now India is making use of the boundary issue to distort everything in China and to speak ill of her domestic movements.

Concerning China's India policy, Odd Arne Westad writes that as she became more left-ward internally, she tended to see the Indian leadership as more of a successor to the British imperialists. Mao Zedong thought that there was India's hand behind the Tibetan rebellion, and also that India and Nehru wanted to go to war with China.[27]

One important viewpoint Dutt has introduced is the relations between China and the USSR. The first Soviet remark on the Indo-

Chinese relations was made on 9 September, 1959, shortly after the clash at Longju. It was strongly resented by China as it did not criticize India, a successor to an imperialist country, widening the gap between China and the USSR, both socialist countries. Dutt did not ask here if China went to war with India all the same even without her worsening relations with the USSR, or went to war because of the worsening relations, considering India as its ally and easier to beat, and beat first.

Then Nehru set his "Forward Policy" to work on 2 November, 1961. In Zachariah's words it consisted of sending 'adventurous border patrols' by India which he called 'This absurd policy…'.[28] Odd Arne Westad also says that if only India admitted that there is a dispute both in the Western and the Eastern Sectors, and refrained from launching the forward policy, that alone would have averted the war, without damaging India's national honour. Moreover, India has put in startlingly fewer troops with poor weapons and ammunitions and in spite of unfavourable geography. On top of it they acted first, though they refrained from using their air force. It was 'an unnecessary war', he said.[29]

Nehru wrote on 12 October, 1962 that "Till last month NEFA was intact and free from any Chinese aggression except a small village on the border called Longju, which also had been vacated by the Chinese". However, "On the 8th of September, some Chinese forces came down through the Thagla Pass and occupied a mile or two of territory there". Therefore, he said, "We have taken steps to strengthen our position and to try to push the Chinese out" (LCM, 5-530-1). This was the official Indian view. We are, however, astonished to read Nehru winding up this letter by writing that "I am going today to Ceylon for four days. I shall return to Delhi on the 16th of October" (*Ibid.*, 533). This is the result of the concentration of power in one person that we discussed before, at least in the field of foreign policy, who had to take care of everything himself, or who wanted to. We are also led to wonder if Nehru was really serious about the Chinese threat, contrary to what he was writing, or he was of the view that the threat was not much, or that the initiative was still in the Indian hands.

Further, the Indian official view was that "On 10, October 1962, the Chinese attacked the Indian outpost at Dhola" (LCM, 5-531fn23). It further said that "On 20, October 1962, China mounted a massive attack" (*Ibid.*, 534fn2) on both NEFA and Ladakh. Now, we will have to check the validity of those Indian claims.

Notes

1. Yamaguchi, *How Relevant is Gandhi Today*, 57.
2. Gopal, S., *Jawaharlal Nehru*, Vol. 3, 89 fn78.
3. Guha, Ramachandra, *India After Gandhi*, 314, 812-Notes 25.
4. *Ibid.*, 318.
5. *Ibid.*, 313.
6. Garver, J.W., *Protracted Contest*, 59.
7. Maxwell, Neville, *India's China War*, 66-9.
8. Zachariah, Benjamin, *Nehru*, 238.
9. *Ibid.*, 239.
10. *Sardar Patel's Correspondence*, Vol.10, 335-341.
11. *Ibid.*, 342-7.
12. Shankar, V., My Reminiscences of Sardar Patel, II, 138-40.
13. *Sardar Patel's Correspondence*, Vol., 9, 245-6.
14. *Ibid.*, 247.
15. Akbar, M.J., *Nehru*, 501, Tharoor, Shashi, *Nehru*, 209.
16. Zachariah, Benjamin, *Nehru*, 235.
17. *Ibid.*
18. *Ibid.*, 260.
19. Maxwell, Neville, *India's China War*, 122-3.
20. Westad, Odd Arne, *Restless Empire*, 335-345.
21. Maxwell, Neville, *India's China War*, 74.
22. *Ibid.*, 313.
23. *Ibid.*, 246.
24. Dutt, Subimal, *With Nehru in the Foreign Office*, 114.
25. *Ibid.*, 129.
26. Suyin, Han, *Eldest Son*, 289.
27. Westad, Odd Arne, *Restless Empire*, 341-3.
28. Zachariah, Benjamin, *Nehru*, 244.
29. Westad, Odd Arne, *Restless Empire*, 334.

10
India and China Go to War

The 1962 War

In his broadcast to the nation on 22nd October, 1962, already in the midst of fighting on both the East and the West, Nehru described the McMahon Line thus. "Our border with China in the NEFA region is well known and well established from ages past. It is sometimes called the McMahon Line. This line which separates India from Tibet was the line of the high ridges which divided the watershed. This has been acknowledged as the border by history, tradition and treaties long before it was called the McMahon Line."[1] It may be pointed out unfortunately that the Indo-Chinese border has not been as stabilized as the above statement claims. China's claims have made it clear that at least there has been a dispute on the exact location of the boundary. The difference in approach between the two great countries of Asia has finally brought about a war between them if not on a very large scale, and shattered the hope of tens of millions of people, this author included, in Asia and elsewhere to see two different but equally prosperous, people-friendly, and competitive ways of development.

The actual trigger was pulled when India launched its "Forward Policy" toward the end of 1961. According to Maxwell there was 'a crucial meeting' at the Prime Minister's Office (PMO) on 2nd November of that year when it was directed to take Chip Chap in the West.[2] Garver also writes on the desperate Nehru at this point as follows: "Nehru, acting from a position of incredible military weakness and oblivious to the logistic realities of operations in the Himalayas, then ordered Indian forces to advance into disputed areas and clear Chinese forces, though without firing first."[3]

India then recognized Thag-La Ridge, on the western end of the McMahon Line, as a part of the border. They constructed the Dhola Post under the Ridge which was actually north of the Line.[4] If you put the Ridge itself on the Line then the Dhola Post can be placed on the south.

Then at the Defence Ministry in Delhi on 9 September, 1962 it was decided to evict the Chinese quickly. In the absence of Nehru and Morarji Desai overseas, it was practically Defence Minister Krishna Menon's decision.[5] But, the biographer of Krishna Menon writes, Nehru is believed to have said at the Delhi Airport on his way to Madras on 12 October that "I have given orders to the army to throw the Chinese out."[6] Han Suyin's description, which is slightly different, is as follows: "In September, Nehru made a speech in Madras, in which he used the phrase 'throw the Chinese out'. On October 10, he called for military action."[7] Why did such an order come from the Prime Minister himself directly and not from the Defence Minister or the Army Chief of Staff? And why on his way to somewhere, which makes it look casual, sometimes very casual? Did he know that already serious fighting had started by this time?

The 4th Infantry Division of the Indian Army, including the 7th Infantry Brigade, had been placed under B.M. Kaul and his 4th Corps which was newly created to evict the Chinese. On 9 October, about 50 soldiers crossed a river from the Indian side at the Dhola Post under the direct command of Kaul, a Lt-General, with the Brigadier left unoccupied, and took a place called Tseng-jong. This action invited a Chinese counter-offensive on the next day.[8] The Chinese attacked on 20th October, and the 7th Brigade disappeared after heavy fighting. Something similar happened in the Western sector also, but 90 per cent of the Indian casualties and 4,000 POWs occurred in the East.[9]

Nehru was still "confident and not at all apologetic".[10] The reasons for the defeat was that they were outnumbered, and also the Jawans did not want to retreat.[11] Later he would put them in somewhat different words in his *Letters to Chief Ministers*, as we will see. The worst is gone now, he said.[12] Was he correct?

John Dalvi's View

We will describe in a little more detail how the war was actually fought, mainly depending on John Dalvi's *Himalayan Blunder*.

Dalvi was a Brigadier in the Indian Army, and was, as he calls himself, "the only senior officer who was there throughout" in the Eastern Sector.[13]

As he recalls, the Chinese troops invaded the Thag-La Ridge area on 8th September, 1962 and thus set a fire to the fuse. This was the beginning of the "NEFA Reverse". India should have either prepared herself for a fight or to negotiate. 'We did neither'.[14] Since, the first days of independence India stuck to the McMahon Line. China must have seen it as imperialism. Why did not Nehru, a fighter against British imperialism, see it in this way? India concluded a Treaty on Tibet with China on 29 April, 1954. Was it not a good occasion to define the boundary together with China? There was no other seed for friction between the two countries. As of 1958 the Chinese maps included considerable Indian territory as theirs. Zhou said they were old maps and a new survey was necessary to rectify them. India just believed it. The choices before Nehru were either to rearm against both China and Pakistan, or to be friendly with China and to industrialize herself. But by 1962 we were not ready either for fighting or talking.[15]

1959 was the turning point.[16] At the end of March the Dalai Lama and his party sought and got asylum in India, which must have been seen as unfriendly in China. Nehru conducted India's diplomacy only with the advice of Krishna Menon and a few officials from the MEA.[17] But, they built the Dhola Post without any back-up defence mechanism in May to June 1962. The 4th Infantry Division was meant for the plains but was mobilized this time without any acclimatization.[18] It does not snow much on the Tibetan side, but on the Indian side there is heavy precipitation. We had to depend on the parachutes for materials, but they often do not open. Trucks were far easier to use in Tibet. We might have been wiser to abandon the Post. Thag-La is said to be on the Chinese side of the Line. K.S. Thimayya, the former Army Chief of Staff up to April 1961, was saying that such a Post was useless, and a large formation may be deployed only up to Bomdi-La way down below on the Indian side. The Government started the "Forward Policy" only after Thimayya and others were retired.[19]

Among the many mistakes Nehru had committed, the greatest one to Dalvi was to appoint B.M. Kaul as the Commander of the Task

Force (4th Corps) to evict the Chinese in NEFA.[20] "I became the Brigadier of the 7th Infantry Brigade in January 1962, with my Headquarters at Tawang in NEFA, to defend Tawang and the McMahon Line."[21] The Dhola Post naturally attracted the Chinese attention.[22] It was unsound to build a post at such a place, giving the others a good excuse for an attack. The 4th Division to which the 7th Brigade belonged to was "the most experienced infantry formation in North Africa"[23] during the Second World War. However, the only other Brigade of the Division, the 11th, was now far away in Nagaland, and there was no defence in depth in the NEFA. If the 11th Brigade had been at Bomdi-La the situation would have been very different.[24]

On 8 September, 1962 about 600 troops of the Chinese army attacked the Dhola Post. Nehru repeatedly demanded that the situation be returned to the pre-8 September condition since then. But it was the Indian side that had built the Post. On 14 September it was decided to evict the Chinese, • this time in the presence of the Defence Minister, but the Prime Minister and Morarji Desai were abroad.[25] On 22 September, it was again decided to evict the Chinese even in the absence of the Defence Minister.[26] The 40-ft wide Namka Chu river at Dhola became the *defacto* military boundary between the two sides.

The biggest question was if Kaul had not been appointed the Corp Commander would there still have been a fighting? His was an appointment by Nehru. On 5, October Kaul, without informing the GOC of the Division or Dalvi himself who was on the spot as the Brigadier, moved the 7th Brigade from Lumpu up to Dhola.[27] He was solely responsible for this act, thus placing the Brigade into the net in which the Chinese were waiting. The Government of India knew that they were not in a position to retreat because of the political pressure. They were, as Dalvi saw, the only group of politicians in the world who did not know the war. On 9th October the army occupied a small village, • there was a counter-offensive, to great casualties to both. China was waiting to have an excuse that they have attacked for self-defence. If there had not been this battle there would not have been the Chinese offensive of 20th October either.[28] The Defence Minister gave his direction that 1st November was the deadline for the Indian side to evict the Chinese.[29] It was possible to anticipate on 19th October how the Chinese would move the next day.[30] You would not be able to call the Chinese offensive a stab from the back because it was not actually from the back. The Indian army had to fight without wire, without anti-personnel mines, and without fire.

At the Chinese offensive of 20th October, in Dalvi's words, "the 7th Brigade expired"[31] , and he himself became a prisoner. As he recalls, from 8 September to 20 October "I was not given a single operation order in writing."[32]

Dalvi also recalls that Menon was the only person who understands the world and the Non-Alignment policy, and Nehru depended only on his advice for his diplomacy.[33] Menon looked at Pakistan as the main enemy and was against the "Forward Policy."[34]

Nehru on the War

After studying the 1962 war on the basis of Brigadier Dalvi's views, we now pay attention to a few notable things which Nehru wrote in his letter of 22nd December, 1962. It was probably the last one of substance in his *Letters to Chief Ministers*. It was the time when major battles had been already fought, especially in the Eastern sector which is NEFA, and had ended unfavourably for India.

Nehru said in the beginning that "The reaction in the country, however, was most heartening." He was, of course, not at all happy at the situation. But he must have become more or less enthusiastic to see waves of expression of mass support to the Government and to him which he had not been able to create so far for the reasons we have seen already.

Then he mentioned a couple of factors as the cause of India's military reversal. One was that "It seems to me that the major reasons for our reverses were the choice of the terrain on which we had to fight the Chinese." For him, compared to this, "it could not be said that lack of winter clothing or modern arms had any very great effect." But in fact many Indian soldiers were severely handicapped by their summer clothing, light shoes and archaic weapons in the high Himalayan hills. Concerning "the choice of the terrain", he seemed to have forgotten that those terrains had been there from the time immemorial, and there could not have been much choice between this terrain and that terrain. It was a matter of preparations or lack of them.

Nehru continued that "A second major disadvantage to our Army was the fact that our forces had been sent rather hurriedly from low altitudes near sea level to an altitude of about 14,000 feet." He was talking of lack of acclimatization. Would it, like the first one, sound reasonable? There had been the same terrains there for years and they had been associated with particular altitude and particular climate which could not have been new to them. Moreover the Indian Army was in a position to choose their own timing to go to war, if they at all had to do so, with ample time for acclimatization. Both of these statements hardly make sense. In short, the Indian troops, or rather the Indian politicians, wanted to fight without being ready, and so in many ways, and perhaps without expecting the counter-offensive of that scale and intensity.

Then who was responsible for the reverses? Again Nehru's views are astonishing. He said, "Some of our Generals have been heavily criticized and have been retired from Service. Many unkind things are said about them without much justification. It was right perhaps that they offered their resignation as honourable men. But the fault was hardly theirs." Mainly it was P.N. Thapar, Army Chief of Staff, and B.M. Kaul, Commander of the 4th Corps, that were criticized and had to be retired among the army generals. So, Nehru was defending them, probably the latter more than the former. But, the top Generals are those who by definition shoulder responsibility. If not, then whose fault was it? "The faults...were of the local Commanders of Brigades and the like who had to decide on the spur of the moment what they should do when they were being overwhelmed by large numbers of the enemy" (SWJN-2, 5-540-6). So, it was people like Dalvi who were responsible for the defeat, people like Dalvi who had not been consulted and who had not received any order in writing. We will also see at the end of this Chapter an example of how they (not necessarily Brigadiers) were side-tracked and their advice not heeded by their superiors, including Nehru himself, or his Defence Minister. Talking of the Defence Minister, Krishna Menon was deposed to the Minister for Defence Production on 31st October, and was relieved of even that on 7th November.

We also wonder why Nehru, with practically no military know-how, although he had experienced some bombing at Barcelona and Chungking, said a final word like this on the causes of the reverses and where the responsibility lay? Should it not be done by the military experts? This is not a question of the civilian control. This is a question of if Nehru and his Ministers had listened to his military advisers and if the latter in turn had listened to the 'Brigadiers' (not a particular one) who were experts on the spot.

In Judith Brown's view, "the harsh truth was that he had not thought that China would ever attack India...".[35] Srinath Raghavan also writes in the *Outlook* Anniversary Number mentioned above that the Indian leadership thought that China would resort to only skirmishes but not more.[36] Perhaps for this reason he says that the Indian Army could not propose any action plan to the Government. But is the idea of no attack on India thinkable at all no matter what India might do? Brown has not taken Nehru's "Forward Policy" into consideration.

There is a Chapter on "Foreign Policy: The Nehru Era" in Bipan Chandra, Mridula Mukherjee and Aditya Mukherjee's book *India Since Independence*, mentioned above. The analysis in this Chapter, by Mridula Mukherjee, seems to be making a similar mistake. It says that there are two kinds of views which hold Nehru responsible. One is that Nehru was 'blinded by sentiment', and the other was the type of Maxwell which says that Nehru 'provoked' China, but both are wrong. The sentiment issue aside, the author thinks that it is true that Nehru provoked China consciously or unconsciously.[37] Perhaps he did much more than that, especially if seen from the Chinese point of view, and took an offensive of a very adventurist nature without reliable information from his intelligence. Therefore, even if, he was 'taken by surprise', he had only himself to blame in not anticipating where the counter-offensive would take place, even in not anticipating it at all. India could well have averted major military clashes. The analysis of this type is thus uncritically partial in favour of Nehru. Was it not true that Nehru from the beginning to the end refused to talk with his Chinese counterpart on the border issue, denying the existence of such an issue?

Maxwell said if only India had taken part in the negotiation, China would have accepted the McMahon Line as the border.[38] Similarly, Odd Arne Westad said that China began to look at India to be on the side of the imperialist camp by 1959, but did not want to go to war with India, and if both sides had a will to negotiate the war would have been averted.[39] Both had given interviews in the above-mentioned *Outlook*.

Concerning China, Nehru's judgement was much nearer the truth. He said, in the same letter, that "there is a wide and growing rift between the Soviet Union and China", and "If India could be humiliated and defeated and perhaps even driven into the other camp of the Western Powers, that would be the end of non-alignment for other countries also, and Russia's policy would have been broken down" (LCM, 5-549, 551). Here Nehru attributes the Indo-Chinese War entirely to China's ambitions, and pays no attention to India's own "forward policy" or her refusal to negotiate. It must have made it difficult for India to change its course in relation with China after Nehru was gone.

Nehru could have asked China if, with all the continuing internal difficulties in China, like the collapse of "Great Leap Forward" already referred to, China had any legitimacy to go to war, any war? He may well have said also that it was because China was not a democratic state that she could do what most of the people could not have liked. Look at the enormous casualties during the Korean War, which continued for three years. When it comes to that, however, the question would also catch hold of India, and perhaps more tightly. For, in spite of being a nation which functions in the name of democracy, the largest democracy in the world, a nation who rose against the British involvement of India without consulting them into their own war, this time they compelled the common people a collision course with a far stronger enemy without knowing, even suspecting so.

We may here listen to the story of an effort by the Defence Minister Krishna Menon to avert war with China, once quoted above from Srinath Raghavan. It was written by Janaki Ram, Menon's grandniece, in her biography of Menon. She does not talk about his political motivation for doing so. It may be that he was more apprehensive of Pakistan than of China. 'As late as July 1962', which meant really late with only a few months left before the fighting began, both Menon and China's Foreign Minister Chen Yi (Chen I) found themselves in Geneva in connection with the Laotian question.

Then, "at the closing of the conference, Chen Yi and Menon met thrice...and the talks were fruitful to the extent that the Chinese agreed to consider them as a process towards a settlement...Chen Yi at the last of these meetings suggested issuing a joint communique, stating that two senior Ministers of the Governments of India and China met, had fruitful discussions on the border issue, and it was intended that such meetings would continue." The Chinese side may have taken their Government's previous approval already, but not the Indian side. Nehru's approval did not reach Geneva before both the Ministers left. Moreover, Nehru did not do enough to defend Menon's work in the face of the right wingers back home, so that "The Chinese felt rebuffed and in the light of criticism Menon encountered, nothing more could be done by him." Menon's ability could not thus be utilized where it might be most useful.[40]

Incidentally, Janaki Ram says of Menon, the Defence Minister, that "His greatest contribution was to set the defence needs of the country on a path of self-reliance", and quotes an army general saying "but for him we would not have had a defence industry."[41]

Meanwhile on the ground, the Chinese announced a unilateral ceasefire and withdrawal of their forces on 21st November, and made a formal proposal including these the next day. It was a fantastic episode that Lal Bahadur Shastri, Minister without Portfolio and his entourage including Kuldip Nayar, only came to know the news at the Delhi Airport through newspapers as they were about to board their plane that very morning of 21st November.[42] India made a counter-proposal that both the forces be withdrawn to the line of 8 September, 1962, which China rejected on 30 December. Nehru "in his reply of 1st January, 1963 urged China to vacate aggression committed by her since 8 September, 1962..." (LCM, 5-561fn5).

Kuldip Nayar, by the way, writes that the Chinese objective was 'humbling India', and by so doing to grasp the hegemony of the Third World into her own hand. At the same time the Soviet camp itself was not united as firmly. Nayar wrote what a pro-Beijing Ambassador from an East European country told him, assuring that it was also the Russian view. He recommended a package political deal between the two, namely the recognition of the McMahon Line by China in return for India's offering a part of Ladakh which has never been charted so far. The idea itself would suggest that the border problem would be easier to solve in the Eastern Sector. Nayar adds that if Nehru had been alone, he would have agreed to this.[43] He does not give the date of this conversation. But it shows how the Indo-Chinese border issue had been internationalized.

S. Gopal writes that Felix Bandaranaike, the Sri Lankan President, while intervening in the conflict, was told by Liu Shaoqi, China's President, that their objective was to destroy the arrogance' of India, and they "had taught India a lesson and, if necessary, they would teach her a lesson again and again."[44] Arrogance was on which side?

Here in Japan we noticed that at least two books in the Japanese language were published and circulated by the Chinese Government publishers for their propaganda in Japan. The first was titled *The Tibetan Question*, published in 1959. This is a collection of a number of short articles and statements not much of substance in themselves except the already mentioned *People's Daily* article "On the Tibetan Revolution and the Philosophy of Nehru". But the second one, *The Sino-Indian Border Question*, 1962, was of much more substance.

It is a collection of the following six documents, if chronologically rearranged, (1) A letter from Zhou En-lai to Nehru *via* G. Parthasarathy, proposing a mutual 20 km withdrawal of both forces, on 7th November 1959. (2) Three questions by the Chinese Foreign Ministry to the Government of India of 26th December, 1959, mentioned above. (3) A statement by the Chinese Government again proposing a mutual 20 km withdrawal on 24 October, 1962, this time in the midst of fierce fighting. (4) *The People's Daily* article "Again on the Nehru's Philosophy", mentioned before. (5) Zhou's letter to some of the Asian and African leaders criticizing India and explaining China's stand dated 15 November, 1962. The war had broken out and some of those leaders, led by Sri Lanka (then Ceylon), were sounding the two countries on the possibility of peaceful solution of the border problem. (6) The Chinese Government's statement of 21 November declaring a ceasefire from the next day and withdrawal of her troops by 20 km. A number of maps are attached to the book.

By contrast, it seems the Government of India did not publish something of their own in Japanese for their propaganda, as China did. Instead, a Japanese journalist translated a relatively small pamphlet called *The Chinesse Threat*, published by the Publications Division, Delhi, in January 1963, into Japanese and got it published in Japan. In this book we may also see seven documents, of which Nehru's letter to Zhou on 26 September, 1959 is the most important, and many maps as Appendices.

There is a Government of India document called *Henderson Brooks—Bhagat Report*, which is not yet open to the public. Maxwell says it is top secret. Nayar's *Between The Lines* contains some extracts from the Report, which seem to criticize the interference in the tactics by the non-military.

Maxwell said in the same *Outlook* Number that one reason why the report had not been opened up was that the Government of India wanted it to be hidden that the Indian Army and especially its 4th Corps Commander M.B. Kaul were not familiar with the situation at the boundary. In spite of that, they had to build a Post at Dhola under the political pressure, without being sure whether it was to the south or to the north of the McMahon Line.[45]

Talking of Dhola, in an article "BJP's Bipolar Behaviour and the Shroud of Secrecy Around the 1962 War" in the *Wire* of 28 March, 2018, Sonia Trikha Shukla said that Henderson Brooks-Bhagat report has remained a classified document till today, but the BJP which has pressed for its early release has been suppressing it at present. One reason is that "Dhola Post was established north of the McMahon Line", a point with far-reaching implications, especially against Nehru, but which had been neglected so far.

S.P.P. Thorat and Nehru

About Nehru's last moment, there is the following episode, rather sad for the Nehruvians, in the last chapter called "The Last Hundred Days" in the memoir *Outside the Archives* by Y.D. Gundevia, a retired ICS. Nehru gave a 45-minite Press Conference on 22 May, 1964, just 5 days before his demise. The last question was he had not nominated his successor. Nehru replied, "I don't think I am passing away that soon". Laughter all around.[46] The author, however, has been impressed by the fact that Nehru did not oppose the use of such expressions like his nominating a successor. Was he not different from Gandhi on this point? From a certain point of time Gandhi made it clear about Nehru's relation to him as his heir. One thing is clear. As Nehru himself wrote in the *Modern Review* a long time ago, he was not at all keen to retire. He must have been with a firm conviction that his work has not been finished. "He cannot rest, for he who rides a tiger cannot dismount."[47]

We will briefly sum up here a memoir of an Indian Army General, who was not in the battle ground of 1962 as was Dalvi and others, but who still experienced much of the tragedy of the Indian Army, and finally met Nehru in a tragic condition.

He was Lt. Gen. S.P.P. Thorat. He wrote *From Reveille to Retreat* in 1986, a quarter of a century after the war. In 1950 he was a Maj. Gen. and Chief of the General Staff (to be distinguished from the Army Chief of Staff, the highest post in the Army). The Army was then divided into three Commands, Southern, Eastern and Western each with the headquarters at Poona, Lucknow and Delhi. The Indian State forces had just been integrated by the efforts of Sardar Patel and V.P. Menon. Thorat was dispatched to Korea as the head of 5,000 Indian soldiers to help negotiate peace.

Back in India, he was made GOC-in-C Eastern Command, under General K.S. Thimayya as the Army Chief of Staff and remained there for four years from 1957 to 1961 when he retired. Including the Naga Hills District, this was the largest Command. He gave thought to the problem of defence of the NEFA himself. It seemed to be easy to come from Tibet to Tawang or Walong *via* a few mountain passes. But the Chinese Army in Tibet, of 8 Divisions each with 14,000 soldiers then, would not be able to attack at the same time, as "no roads were leading to India", and no armour could be used. "Certainly the Chinese advance cannot hope to reach the Brahmaputra valley. At the best it must stop midway in NEFA." As to the Chinese intention to invade India, however, the Government's complaisant attitude looked curious to him.[48]

Thorat anticipated several possible routes of attack, put his idea into a paper, signed it on 8 October, 1959, and submitted it to the Defence Minister *via* Thimayya. It did not claim the attention of Menon and Kaul.[49]

He had an opportunity to meet Nehru soon after the fighting was over. "I saw a haggard-looking Prime Minister sitting at his desk with a vacant expressions (*sic*) on his face...It was indeed a pathetic sight." Thorat showed him his paper. Nehru asked if the Chinese were coming down to the Brahmaputra valley. Thorat answered 'No'.[50] The author wonders which of the two papers was of more importance and of more interest to Nehru at that moment, the Conclusion of the Indian Summary of the *Supplement* shown to him by Mehta and Gopal, or the paper by Thorat ?

Nehru died on 27 May, 1964.

Notes

1. Nehru, *The Essential Writings of Jawaharlal Nehru*, II, 307.
2. Maxwell, Neville, *India's China War*, 233, 505.
3. Garver, J.W., *Protracted Contest*, 80.
4. Maxwell, Neville, *India's China War*, 379.
5. *Ibid.*, 327.
6. Ram, Janaki, *V.K. Krishna Menon*, 129-130.
7. Suyin, Han, *Eldest Son*, 293.
8. Maxwell, Neville, *India's China War*, 366.
9. *Ibid.*, 465, 476.
10. *Ibid.*, 418.
11. *Ibid.*
12. *Ibid.*, 421.
13. Dalvi, John, P., *Himalayan Blunder*, 497.
14. *Ibid.*, 15.
15. *Ibid.*, 149.
16. *Ibid.*, 36.
17. *Ibid.*, 43, 77.
18. *Ibid.*, 56.
19. *Ibid.*, 67.
20. *Ibid.*, 94.
21. *Ibid.*, 118.
22. *Ibid.*, 133.
23. Raghavan, Srinath, *India's War*, 365.
24. Dalvi, John P., *Himalayan Blunder*, 144.
25. *Ibid.*, 200.
26. *Ibid.*, 228-9.
27. *Ibid.*, 262.
28. *Ibid.*, 300.
29. *Ibid.*, 330.
30. *Ibid.*, 336-7, 339.
31. *Ibid.*, 375.
32. *Ibid.*, 440.
33. *Ibid.*, 462.
34. *Ibid.*, 459, 461.
35. Brown, Judith, *Nehru*, 162.
36. Raghavan, Srinath, *Outlook* Anniversary Number.
37. Bipan Chandra, Mridula and Aditya Mukherjee, *India Since Independence*, 210-6.
38. Maxwell, Neville, *Outlook* Anniversary Number.
39. Westad, Odd Arne, *Outlook* Anniversary Number.

40. Ram, Janaki, *V.K. Krishna Menon*, 70.
41. *Ibid.*, 116, 138.
42. Nayar, Kuldip, *Between the Lines*, 211.
43. *Ibid.*, 174-5.
44. Gopal, S., *Jawaharlal Nehru*, Vol. 3, 230 fn150.
45. Maxwell, Neville, *Outlook* Anniversary Number.
46. Gundevia, D., *Outside the Archives*, 418.
47. Nehru, *The Essential Writings of Jawaharlal Nehru*, II, 646.
48. Thorat, S.P.P., *From Reveille to Retreat*, 191-5.
49. *Ibid.*, 200.
50. *Ibid.*, 215-7.

Epilogue

While China was giving support to almost all the anti-Indian armed struggle in South Asia between 1962 and 1979, Deng Xiaoping changed the policy drastically.[1] This established a condition for restoring peaceful relations between the two. The exchange of key personnel began with the visit by Atal Behari Vajpayee, India's Foreign Minister in the Janata Party Government, to China in February 1979, although he hurried home as China invaded Vietnam. But Vajpayee's visit was returned by the visit of China's Foreign Minister Huang Hua to India in June 1981.

Then India's Prime Minister Rajiv Gandhi (Nehru's grandson) and China's counterpart Li Peng visited each other's country in December 1988 and December 1991, respectively. After that the exchanges of VIPs have been numerous. At the same time Peace and Tranquility Treaty was concluded in 1993, and Strategic and Cooperative Partnership was established in 2005. Serious conferences on the border issue were resumed in December 1981[2], like the 15th Round of Special Representative (SRs) talks on the Boundary Question, in January 2012. The present President of China Xi Jinping visited India in September 2014. The recent Indo-Chinese summit will be taken up shortly.

India's Journalist N. Ram, of *The Hindu*, known for his keen interest in the Indo-Chinese border issue, made a special study of it about thirty years ago, including a visit to China. His three-part article in *The Hindu* of 29 June to 1 July, 1987, titled "A delicate pass in Sino-Indian relations", includes several important points. First, he reported on India's External Affairs Minister N.D. Tiwari's successful China visit in 1987. It preceded Prime Minister Rajiv Gandhi's visit by a year. Tiwari was told by the Chinese that Rajiv's meeting with China's Communist Party General Secretary Zhao Ziyang in New York in 1985 was already a success. Second, Ram wrote that A.P. Venkateswaran, India's Foreign Secretary, advised his Government against the proposed promotion of the then NEFA to the State of Arunachal Pradesh at least three times as it would worsen the relation between the two. But the Government had its way at the end of 1986. Third, Ram also said that a senior Chinese Communist Party official told him informally that it would be more difficult to solve the border issue in the Eastern Sector where India occupied 90,000 square kilometres out of which 80,000 belonged to Arunachal Pradesh. According to this official, the Chinese side said at an official meeting that China would concede in the Western Sector, so India should do the same in the East. This is contrary to what Zhou En-lai was supposed to imply in his communication with Nehru and was quoted by Guha as mentioned before, though Nehru did not seem to study it seriously. But the promotion of NEFA to Arunachal Pradesh shows that India was not ready to concede or exchange territories.

The author could not believe his eyes when he saw the Chinese Ambassador to India telling the TV camera in India that the whole Arunachal Pradesh was a part of China. There was little doubt that he was speaking his confirmed opinion. Otherwise how could he have said so in the week preceding President Hu Jintao's official India visit? Moreover, it was the Children's Day in India, namely Nehru's birthday, on 14 November, 2006. A voice was raised in India demanding the Ambassador's recall who was rather notorious in matters like that. But it showed that the border dispute still remains unresolved.

In this book a major emphasis has been placed on how India and China went to war, and what was the role Nehru played in it. The historic significance of the 1962 Indo-Chinese War lies not in the fact of fighting itself between the two big countries, but in the fact that the PRC, which would have remained more or less within her own domain if there had been no such war, was in fact drawn by India, particularly Nehru, consciously or unconsciously, into the world of South Asia, an entirely new environment for her. 1962 was followed in a few years' time by the Indo-Pakistani War of 1965, and a few more years later by the Bangladesh War of 1971. All the talks of China encircling India with its naval and other maritime means, of naval exercises even in as far away as the Baltic Sea, of India encircling China in a reverse way with the Russian help, of the triangular relations of India, China and Japan, with India particularly interested in the possibility of India and Japan cooperating against China politically, economically and strategically, started from China's fresh involvement in the South Asian world starting from 1962, with Nehru saying 'No' to the border negotiations and ordering to evict the Chinese from near its borders. Since Nehru was so persistent in being negative to any negotiations from the beginning, from India's independence and the People's Republic of China's establishment, since even after Nehru it was mostly the "dynasty" that was in power in India, and since he was so genuinely respected, the later generations of India's politicians and bureaucrats were strongly discouraged from trying to open a new gate to negotiate with China on the boundary issue. New negotiation has been almost impossible. And how long more do we have to wait?

Doubtless there had been a developing connection between the PRC and Pakistan. It had become so close that China sent ultimatums, not one but two, to India, on 8 and 16 September, 1965, at the time of the Indo-Pakistani War. But such a depth, and China's partiality towards Pakistan, would have been unthinkable if there had been no 1962. That close Sino-Pakistani ties came to be known as the all-weather relations. The author had a glimpse of it in 1999 when he was in Pakistan attending an international seminar, and saw with astonishment the Chinese Ambassador to Pakistan, alone among all the Ambassadors from the countries of the seminar participants, invited to the closing ceremony to make a speech.

The latest Indo-Chinese summit at the time of writing was held at Wuhan in central China for over 9 hours on 27 and 28 April, 2018 between the Chinese President and the Indian Prime Minister. It so happened that 27 April was the day when the North Korean Chairman visited South Korea, even by a few metres, to meet his counterpart of South Korea. Its implication for the Far East must have been greater than that of the Indo-Chinese summit for South Asia, but the latter was also important. The economic relations between the two, at least on the surface, have been smoothly growing. For example the Third Annual Meeting of the China-sponsored Asian Infrastructural Investment Bank (AIIB) was held in Mumbai at the end of June 2018. The investment by the Bank in India alone amounts to about 30 per cent of the total and has surpassed the case of any of the 86 other member countries.

There was an interview of Shivshankar Menon, India's retired veteran diplomat and former Foreign Secretary, on this summit on the *Wire* of 2 May by Devirupa Mitra. Menon said in reply to one of the questions that among the big things China immediately could do for the better relations between the two countries are, neutrality between India and Pakistan, trade imbalances, maritime security, and "Both of us need a stable periphery, if we need to concentrate on our domestic economic development." On the periphery we can cooperate in Afghanistan, he added. Very good. We must notice, however, that for even a diplomat of Shivshankar Menon's career it was perhaps not possible to raise the boundary issue in this connection.

There is one more thing Menon may or may not have commented upon, and it is the "One Belt, One Road" policy of China, or of President Xi Jinping. The adversarial relation of India and Pakistan means that there is an adversarial element in this policy also. Thus, while India remains outside this concept and is taking Japan's help in building up the Mumbai-Ahmedabad Corridor, China is building up Sinkiang-Karachi Corridor in Pakistan. A million Dollar, or RMB, or Rupee question here will be, are they going to be developed in a way that the present disparities, not only in the peripheries but more in the heavily population-concentrated areas, will be reduced significantly. And here we must also keep in mind the Nehruvian conception of development within democratic framework, probably the greatest of all the legacies left by Nehru.

Notes

1. Garver, J.W., *Protracted Contest*, 19.
2. *Ibid.*, 104.

Bibliography

Akbar, M.J. (2002). *Nehru*, Roli Books.

Austin, Granville (1966). *The Indian Constitution: Cornerstone of a Nation*, Clarendon Press.

Balatchandirane, G. (2007). "India's BRICS ambitions, human capital and Japanese lessons", Rajaram Panda and Yoo Fukazawa, eds., *India and Japan in Search of Global Roles*, Promilla and Co.

Bipan Chandra (2012). *The Writings of Bipan Chandra* (edited by Aditya Mukherjee), Orient Blackswan.

Bipan Chandra, Mridula Mukherjee, Aditya Mukherjee (2008). *India Since Independence*, Revised and Updated, Penguin.

Brown, Judith (2003). *Nehru*, Oxford University Press.

Dalvi, John P. (1968). *Himalayan Blunder*, Thacker.

Dreze, Jean and Amartya Sen (1995). *India: Economic Development and Social Opportunity*, Oxford University Press.

Dreze, Jean and Amartya Sen (2013). *An Uncertain Glory: India and its Contradictions*, Penguin.

Dutt, Subimal (1977). *With Nehru in the Foreign Office*, Minerva.

An EPW team (1989). "Centennial appraisal of Nehru legacy: Report on a Seminar", *EPW*, 3 June.

Frank, Katherine (2001). *Indira: The Life of Indira Nehru Gandhi*, HarperCollins.

Gandhi, M.K., *Collected Works of Mahatma Gandhi* (CWMG), vols. 1-100.

Gandhi, Rajmohan, *Patel: A Life*, Navajivan Publishing House.

Garver, John W. (2001). *Protracted Contest; Sino-Indian Rivalry in the Twentieth Century*, University of Washington Press.

Gopal, S. (1975)-84. *Jawaharlal Nehru: A Biography*, 3 vols., Jonathan Cape.

Government of China (1959). *The Tibetan Question* (in Japanese), Foreign Languages Press.

Government of China (1962). *The Sino-Indian Border Question* (in Japanese), Foreign Languages Press.

Guha, Ramachandra (2007). *India After Gandhi: The History of the World's Largest Democracy*, Picador India.

Gundevia, Y.D. (1984). *Outside the Archives*, Sangam Books.

Henderson Brooks-Bhagat, A *Report* (unpublished).

Hirashima, Shigemochi, Hisaya Oda and Yuko Tsujita (eds.)(2011). *Inclusiveness in India: A Strategy for Growth and Equality*, IDE-JETRO

Iyengar, Uma and Lalitha Zachariah (eds.) (2011). *Together They Fought: Gandhi-Nehru Correspondence 1921-1948*, Oxford University Press.

Jha, Prem Shankar (1996). *Kashmir 1947: Rival Versions of History*, Oxford University Press.

Joshi, P.C. (1996). *Mahatma Gandhi: The New Economic Agenda*, Har-Anand.

Krishna, B. (1995). *Sardar Vallabhbhai Patel: India's Iron Man*, Indus.

Malik, Dipak (2013). *Gandhi aur Nehru* (in Hindi), Rajkamal Prakashan.

Maxwell, Neville (1970). *India's China War*, Pantheon Books.

Menon, V.P. (1961). *The Story of the Integration of the Indian States*, Orient Longmans.

Nayar, Kuldip (2006). *Scoop!: Inside Stories from the Partition to the Present*, HarperCollins.

Nayar, Kuldip (2014). *Between the Lines*, Konark Publishers.

Nehru, Jawaharlal (2003). *The Essential Writings of Jawaharlal Nehru* (edited by S. Gopal and Uma Iyengar), 2 vols., Oxford University Press.

Nehru, Jawaharlal (2004). *An Autobiography*, Penguin.

Nehru, Jawaharlal (2004). *Glimpses of World History*, Penguin.

Nehru, Jawaharlal (2004). *The Discovery of India*, Penguin.

Nehru, Jawaharlal, *Letters to Chief Ministers 1947-1964* (General Editor G. Parthasarathi, LCM), Oxford University Press, 5 vols. 1985-89.

Nehru, Jawaharlal, *Selected Works of Jawaharlal Nehru* (General Editor S. Gopal, SWJN-1), Orient Longman, 15 vols., 1972-82.

Nehru, Jawaharlal, *Selected Works of Jawaharlal Nehru, Second Series* (General Editor S. Gopal, SWJN-2), Jawaharlal Nehru Memorial Fund, 1984.

Outlook, 22 October (2012). Fiftieth Anniversary Number of the 1962 War.

Patel, Maniben (2001). *Inside Story of Sardar Patel—The Diary of Maniben Patel: 1936-50*, Vision Books.

Patel, Sardar, 1971-74. *Sardar Patel's Correspondence 1945-50*, (Edited by Durga Das), 10 vols., Navajivan.

Raghavan, Srinath (2016). *India's War: The Making of Modern South Asia 1939-1945*, Penguin.

Ram, Janaki (1997). *V.K. Krishna Menon: A Personal Memoir*, Oxford University Press.

Rao, V.K.R.V. (1971). *Nehru's Legacy*, Popular.

Shankar, V. (1974). *My Reminiscences of Sardar Patel*, 2 vols., MacMillan.

Sheean, Vincent (1960). *Nehru: The Years of Power*, Curtis Brown.

Singh, R.N.P. (2015). *Nehru: A Troubled Legacy*, Wisdom Tree.

Suyin, Han (1994). *Eldest Son: Zhou Enlai and the Making of Modern China, 1898-1976*, Jonathan Cape.

Tharoor, Shashi (2003). *Nehru: The Invention of India*, Penguin.

Thorat, S.P.P. (1986). *From Reville to Retreat*, Allied.

Westad, Odd Arne (2012). *Empire: China and the World Since 1750*, The Bodley Head.

Wilson, Dick (1984). *Chou: The Story of Zhou Enlai 1898-1976*, Hutchinson.

Yamaguchi, Hiroichi (2006). *Japan*, National Book Trust, India.

Yamaguchi, Hiroichi (2015). *How Relevant is Gandhi Today: A Japanese View*, Concept Publishing Co. (P) Ltd., New Delhi.

Zachariah, Benjamin (2004). *Nehru*, Roli.

Index